A project of South Florida Keswick Convention

For Such a Time as This

Raymond Anglin,
Clyde A. Bailey
and
Horace Ward

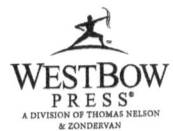

WESTBOW
PRESS®
A DIVISION OF THOMAS NELSON
& ZONDERVAN

Copyright © 2018 Raymond Anglin, Clyde A. Bailey and Horace Ward.

All rights reserved. No part of this book may be used or reproduced by any means, graphic, electronic, or mechanical, including photocopying, recording, taping or by any information storage retrieval system without the written permission of the author except in the case of brief quotations embodied in critical articles and reviews.

WestBow Press books may be ordered through booksellers or by contacting:

WestBow Press
A Division of Thomas Nelson & Zondervan
1663 Liberty Drive
Bloomington, IN 47403
www.westbowpress.com
1 (866) 928-1240

Because of the dynamic nature of the Internet, any web addresses or links contained in this book may have changed since publication and may no longer be valid. The views expressed in this work are solely those of the author and do not necessarily reflect the views of the publisher, and the publisher hereby disclaims any responsibility for them.

Any people depicted in stock imagery provided by Getty Images are models, and such images are being used for illustrative purposes only. Certain stock imagery © Getty Images.

THE HOLY BIBLE, NEW INTERNATIONAL VERSION®, NIV® Copyright © 1973, 1978, 1984, 2011 by Biblica, Inc.® Used by permission. All rights reserved worldwide.

ISBN: 978-1-9736-4203-9 (sc)
ISBN: 978-1-9736-4202-2 (e)

Library of Congress Control Number: 2018912060

Print information available on the last page.

WestBow Press rev. date: 10/24/2018

Contents

Foreword vii
Acknowledgements ix
Chapter 1   Thank God for Keswick! 1
            Gerry O. Gallimore
Chapter 2   Full Salvation: More Than a Song 9
            David Corbin
Chapter 3   Keswick: A Family Affair 17
            Launa Corbin
Chapter 4   Keswick Convention and Spiritual Growth 21
            Richard Heron
Chapter 5   Immigration: Bane and Blessing
            (Implications for South Florida Keswick) 37
            Rev. Dr. Raymond Anglin
Chapter 6   The Impact of Music on the Keswick Convention .. 45
            Reginald G. Smith
Chapter 7   Empowered to Forgive: Forgiving Myself 67
            Kate Quelch
Chapter 8   Keswick: Effectiveness and Relevance 75
            Clyde A. Bailey
Epilogue   South Florida Keswick Convention 85
            Statement of Faith
Current Board Members 87

Foreword

The celebration of Anniversaries offers us the opportunity to come together for fellowship and enjoyment as well as invites us to pause for reflection, introspection and projection.

For the South Florida Keswick Convention, this means reflecting on the past sixteen years since its inception in 2002, engaging in honest and realistic personal and communal introspection and evaluation and recommitting to an unfolding future as we plan and make projections to follow where these will lead us.

We are indeed very thankful to the Almighty God for the abundance of blessings throughout these sixteen years. For the vision that has kept us focused, the faithful and bold leadership we have experienced and the vibrant fellowship into which we have grown and continue to enjoy.

This publication is not merely another thing we do for Anniversary but it represents one of our very special "offerings" as we express our thanks to God who has remained faithful to us and to our brothers and sisters in the various congregations here in South Florida.

It will provide the back-drop against which the Convention was conceived, highlighting some of the early growing experiences, while underscoring the foundational tenets which have influenced and inspired its growth.

This publication recognizes that the Church does not exist in a vacuum but that it is integral to the real lives of people and that which affects the local congregation, affects the Convention. So, two very important subjects were explored i.e. the phenomenon of Migration and the impact of Music. It also appreciates the impact that the Keswick Convention has had and continues to have on individuals who attend each year and how this has strengthened their faith and witness.

In addition to this, there is an insightful and very relevant evaluation of the ministry of the Convention during these fifteen years, posing heart searching questions we all need to answer as we embark on the next chapter of life together.

We hope that as we read this book, we will share pride in being an integral part of what God has been doing through our South Florida Keswick Convention and recommit ourselves to being actively involved in its continuing mission.

Rev. Dr. Raymond Anglin
Vice-Chairman
South Florida Keswick Convention Board

Acknowledgements

> *I always thank my God for you because of his grace given you in Christ Jesus. For in him you have been enriched in every way—with all kinds of speech and with all knowledge—God thus confirming our testimony about Christ among you. Therefore you do not lack any spiritual gift as you eagerly wait for our Lord Jesus Christ to be revealed. He will also keep you firm to the end, so that you will be blameless on the day of our Lord Jesus Christ. (1 Corinthians 1:4–8, NIV)*

In God's name, we give thanks for the grace given in Jesus Christ by the Holy Spirit, that gave birth to the vision of the South Florida Keswick Council to embark on this historic book project. This group of faithful servants of the Servant One, remain passionately engaged in ways to enrich the Body of Jesus Christ gathered in every local congregation here in South Florida and this book project is part of that movement.

We must acknowledge the spiritual gifts of all those communities who have in myriad ways 'raised up' those who have contributed in every which way to this publication. As you eagerly read through each chapter herein, celebrate the unique perspectives of all the contributors lived out among the communities who nurtured them along the way.

At a time like this join too in celebrating how this project is a direct result of so many partners over the years; the sermons of the Annual Convention preachers, to Ministry Partners and the incredible generosity of business and untold volunteers. All those partners have helped to make the one who is Light to 'shine' in the most innovative and real ways.

We humbly say thanks to our beloved wives Pat (Clyde), Marcia (Horace) and Pauline (Ray) for your amazing support and encouragement as we labored on this project. We are grateful for your understanding and your suggestions. You ladies are members of a premium club of super special wives.

Thanks to each contributor for sharing your thoughts and perspectives and for trusting us to represent you well. We appreciate your patience in ensuring that the finished product would be something that is worthy of your integrity and commitment to the ideals of the Keswick movement worldwide.

Finally, to you the reader, thank you for engaging the Word being proclaimed through this publication. After you have read, marked, learnt and inwardly digested this 'gift' in your hands go into the world and let Jesus Christ be known so that others come to follow him in these times and for generations to come.

> *Blessed Lord, who caused all holy Scriptures to be written for our learning: Grant us so to hear them, read, mark, learn, and inwardly digest them, that we may embrace and ever hold fast the blessed hope of everlasting life, which you have given us in our Savior Jesus Christ; who lives and reigns with you and the Holy Spirit, one God, for ever and ever. Amen.*
>
> The Book of Common Prayer, Second Sunday in Advent in the Anglican Church

Chapter 1

Thank God for Keswick!
Gerry O. Gallimore

Yes, thank God for Keswick! It would be almost impossible for me to adequately quantify the profound influence that Keswick ministry has had on my life. It all began in Jamaica in 1958 when my cousin Olga Coke invited several young people from Bethel Baptist Church (Half-Way-Tree, Kingston) to attend the Mandeville Keswick in July. We were accommodated at Jamaica Bible School in what was known as the "house party." The morning Bible readings were held at the Methodist chapel, and the evening meetings were at Ridgemount United Church.

Dr. Stephen Olford, pastor of Calvary Baptist Church, was the speaker that year. The opening night will never be forgotten by any of us who were present. Dr. Olford spoke under great anointing of the Holy Spirit. The place was filled with the convicting presence and power of the Holy Spirit. I was one of scores of people who remained for an "after-meeting," weeping in brokenness before the Lord. Something very special happened in my life that night; the Holy Spirit cleansed and filled our surrendered lives.

By the end of that Keswick week, my spiritual life was at an entirely new level of closeness to the Lord. I felt sensitivity to His will and empowerment and excitement for Christian living. In that "house party," there were about twenty of us young people. Some were from Bethel Baptist Church, and some were from Galilee

Gospel Hall. We forged lasting friendships that week and went back to Kingston on fire for the Lord. My life has never been the same.

In my spirit, I can still hear Stephen Olford expounding on the "exchanged life."

> I have been crucified with Christ and I no longer live, but Christ lives in me. The life I now live in the body, I live by faith in the Son of God, who loved me and gave himself for me. (Galatians 2:20 NIV)

His anointed, soul-searching message is still ringing in my ears:

> Every valley shall be filled in, every mountain and hill made low. The crooked places shall become straight, the rough ways smooth. (Luke 3:5–6 NIV)

Thank God for Keswick and God's ministering servants who faithfully and fearlessly proclaimed the truth that sets men free! From 1958 onward, Mandeville Keswick became an annual fixture in my life.

In those early years in Jamaica, the young people who became infected with the "Keswick virus" simply couldn't get enough of the Keswick teachings. We bought the Keswick books, sang the Keswick hymns, and listened to the Keswick tapes from the preachers in our local conventions and from the library of sermon tapes of the mother Keswick Convention in England.

We feasted our souls on teachings about the deeper life, the Lordship of Christ, the victorious Christian life, sin in the lives of believers, and missions. We sat at the feet of great men of God from overseas like Dr. Stephen Olford, Dr. Sidlow Baxter, Dr. Alan Redpath, Dr. Francis Dixon, Dr. Paul Rees, Dr. Harold Okengay, Dr. Paul Smith, Dr. Alec Motyer, and others from England. In time, Keswick in Jamaica started inviting capable brethren from the Caribbean—Dr. Sam G. Hines, Dr. Wingrove Taylor, Dr. Burchell Taylor, and Dr. Rex Major to name a few—to man the Keswick platforms.

In 1961, through the leadership of distinguished brethren like Mr. Harold Wildish, Rev. David Clark, Rev. Cleve Grant, Mr. George DaCosta, the Kingston Keswick Convention was started. Ardenne High School Hall was the night venue, and Webster Memorial Church was the morning Bible reading venue. I transferred my allegiance from the Mandeville Convention to the new Kingston Keswick Convention.

In that first Kingston Convention, under the anointed preaching of Dr. Stephen Olford, I felt and responded publicly to the call of God on my life for the Christian ministry, which eventually led me into my life's work with Youth for Christ. In time, I was given the privilege of becoming a member of the Kingston Keswick Council and served alongside outstanding Christian leaders, including Dr. Cleve Grant, Sis. Kathleen McFarlane, and Brother George Webster have gone to be with the Lord.

I thank God for the indelible, uplifting, enriching, and consistent impact and input of Keswick on my life over the past fifty-eight years. Each year, I look forward with eager anticipation for the next Keswick Convention. What blessed memories of the "all-one-in-Christ-Jesus's fellowship," the animated singing, and the "holy ground" experiences that Ridgemount United Church in Mandeville and Ardenne High School Hall and Boulevard Baptist Church in Kingston represent!

In 1989, my wife, Sonia, and our three children relocated to Florida to better serve YFC ministries in North America, South America, and the Caribbean. I was area director for YFCI/Americas. After a stint of six years (1990–1996), serving YFC as its international president from its head office in Singapore, Sonia and I returned to Florida, serving YFCI as its international ambassador, while also serving Metropolitan Baptist Church as its pastor.

In 2001 under the leadership of the Holy Spirit, a number of us pastors in South Florida with Caribbean roots began to meet for prayer and to seek God about starting a South Florida Keswick Convention. There was great unity and conviction for the launch of this ministry.

In 2002, the first South Florida Keswick Convention was held at Sierra Norwood Calvary Baptist Church. Dr. Burchell Taylor of Bethel Baptist Church in Kingston was the speaker. I have had the honor of serving as council chairman since the inception.

Capable Christian speakers such as Dr. Burchell Taylor, Dr. David Larsen, Dr. Al Whittinghill, Rev. Hainsley Griffith, Dr. Rex Major, Dr. Sam Vassell, Dr. Raymond Chin, Dr. Stephen Clark, Rev. Kevin Smith, Rev. Everard Allen, Dr. Joel Edwards, Dr. Edward Foggs, Dr. Stuart Briscoe, and Dr. Marcus Davidson have served South Florida Keswick over the past sixteen years with great blessings for God's people. In this way, we are ensuring that the blessings of Keswick continue for our generation and will be available under God to bless upcoming generations.

One of the outstanding features of our South Florida Keswick Convention is the music of our hundred-voice Keswick Choir! This choir is made up of folks from participating churches who enthusiastically give their time and talent for rehearsals and for ministry during each year's convention. God has blessed our convention with a talented, committed, and motivated choir director and gifted instrumentalists who contribute glorious and inspiring choral presentations and congregational hymns.

Since the first year, the South Florida Keswick Convention program has been held in May after the Mother's Day celebration. The main convention sessions are held over four nights: Wednesday, Thursday, Friday, and the grand finale on Sunday night. Some years, we have had lunch-hour meetings on Thursday and Friday in different locations across the South Florida region. On Saturday morning, there is a leaders' prayer breakfast.

For the South Florida Keswick Convention, 2016 was a significant year. A special ladies meeting was held on Thursday morning. The renowned speaker, Mrs. Jill Briscoe, was the wife of the convention speaker. The impact and success of this meeting has led the council to seriously consider adding it to the convention calendar. Over the years, cooperating churches have included the dates for Keswick in their church calendars as part of their church agendas.

From the very outset, the South Florida Keswick Council has been made up of pastors of churches from various denominations. Pastors do not come "representing" their churches or denominations in the sense of being appointed by their church or denomination. They play a personal role and support the "all one in Christ Jesus" ecumenical fellowship for the building of the kingdom through the deeper life emphasis of Keswick.

Occasionally, someone who is not a pastor is added to the council because of his or her special skills. God has blessed the South Florida Keswick Council with a delightfully bonded group of leaders who enjoy each other's company, trust each other, and are committed to the Keswick mission.

The council meets about eight times each year for prayer, planning, and execution. We meet for breakfast one Friday each month at the home of a council member. The wife prepares a full breakfast for each meeting, which is followed by a rigorous business session.

Deep friendships have been forged by council members who share pulpit and support events in each other's churches and stand in support of each other whenever necessary. One of the rich blessings of my life is having these brothers and sisters to serve with. They pray for me and stand with me in my times of crisis. Without a doubt, it is the warm atmosphere of unity, trust, fellowship, and commitment among the Keswick Council that has been responsible for the continuance, growth, and blessing of the South Florida Keswick Convention.

Funding for each year's convention has been and remains a challenge, but thanks be to God, under His blessing and through the faithfulness of His people, each year's budget has been met! We have four areas of income to meet our budget.

- We produce a program booklet for each convention with small ads from cooperating churches. The fee for those ads helps cover the cost of printing the program booklet.

- In May, we have a "pulpit exchange" between the pastors on our council who agree to give the honoraria to the Keswick budget. This helps cover incidental expenses.
- Each year, a commercial organization helps sponsor the Saturday morning leaders' breakfast.
- Primarily, the council depends on the faithful and generous support of God's people through the offerings in each night meeting to cover the main expenses of the convention.

The congregation is told on the opening night what the challenge is. Each night, they are kept abreast of the progress. An appeal is made on the closing night for whatever the deficit is at that point. Thanks be to God for His blessing and for the generous support of attendees—the budget has always been met! The council exercises careful financial stewardship and ensures that all expenses (airfare, hotel, meals, and honorarium for the speaker and his wife, printing, and promotional costs) are met. The finances of South Florida Keswick Council are audited each year by a highly qualified Christian auditor.

Over the years, the council has developed guidelines for its operation and for the selection of speakers. These guidelines have proven extremely valuable for maintaining consistency in operation. They are also useful for the orientation of new council members and as a basis for the annual financial audit.

It has been the policy of South Florida Keswick to select a mission project for partnership at each year's convention. The idea is to be a blessing to a worthy Christian ministry by providing exposure for that ministry through a presentation at the Saturday morning leaders' breakfast and by making a financial contribution from the council to that ministry. Over the years, such exposure and financial support has been given to United Theological College of the West Indies, Jamaica Theological Seminary, Speaking Hands, Choose Life International, Hope Women's Centers, Love Protects, Regent College of the Caribbean, and others.

One of the big challenges that South Florida Keswick Council faces is finding a way to attract young people to the convention. The desire is real, and the discussions have been intense. We have invited youth pastors to join the council, and we have included outstanding youth choirs that often perform excellently and leave immediately after their performance.

Since 2015, we have devoted Friday night to full youth participation (with the exception of the notices, offering, and message). This has produced encouraging results that we hope will inspire some of these young people to attend the other nights. We have also begun a process to bring younger leaders on to the council. We want to significantly increase the blessings of Keswick to more young people without diminishing the enthusiasm and support of the majority audience.

Over the years, I have had the privilege of being the main speaker at conventions in Barbados, Trinidad, Jamaica, and Grand Cayman. I was one of three speakers at the South Florida Keswick Convention of 2004.

I thank God for the indelible, uplifting, enriching, and consistent impact and input of Keswick in my life over the past fifty-eight years. Each year, I look forward to the next Keswick Convention! The memories are blessed, the fellowship is rich and priceless, the singing is heavenly, and the theme—"All One in Christ Jesus"—is timeless. The past fifteen years in South Florida have captured and honored the rich heritage and character of Keswick Convention. Each year, the convention reaches a growing congregation that eagerly looks forward to superb, expository Bible-based sermons that serve to strengthen Christians and honor our Lord.

To God be the glory for His full salvation!

The Mandeville Keswick Convention, located in the middle of Jamaica, is the oldest Keswick Convention outside of England. It was the first overseas Keswick convention, started in 1900, and has maintained an unbroken history to the present time.

Who Is Gerry Gallimore?

Rev. Dr. Gerald Gallimore has been involved in ministry for more than fifty years. A veteran of Youth for Christ (YFC), Gerry has served as national director of Jamaica YFC, area director for YFC International/Americas, and president of Youth for Christ International. Until recently, he was ambassador-at-large for YFCI. In addition, Gerry was senior pastor at the Metropolitan Baptist Church in South Florida for many years before retiring from full-time ministry in 2007. Gerry has been a world-renowned conference speaker and evangelist and Bible teacher and has ministered in more than ninety countries.

Gerry is a founding member of South Florida Keswick and has been the chairman of the board since its inception. He holds an MA from the Denver Theological Seminary and an honorary doctor of divinity degree from Caribbean Graduate School of Theology.

He and his wife, Sonia, have been married for fifty-four years and have three adult children, thirteen grandchildren, and three great-grandchildren.

Chapter 2

Full Salvation: More Than a Song
David Corbin

On Thursday, May 1, 1873, two young Anglican clergymen were among sixteen people who met in the West End of London. The clergymen, Evan Hopkins and E.W. Moore, were profoundly impressed by what they heard at that meeting. A year later, Moore testified at a gathering in Oxford that he was shown things he had never seen before—and that he yielded them and himself to God.

In *These Sixty Years: The Story of the Keswick Convention* (1935), Walter Sloan traced the history of the Keswick Convention from that hour when those two young clergymen entered into the fullness of blessing. At a similar meeting the following year in Oxford, Hopkins led another young Anglican clergyman from the north of England into the secret of a holy life. That clergyman, Canon Harford-Battersby, was then the vicar of parishes in St. John's, Keswick, and Cumberland. The canon had for some time been aware of the need for deeper spiritual power in his own life.

One of the first outward results of that convention at Oxford was a much larger convention at Brighton, and that paved the way for the first Convention at Keswick, which took place in 1875 under the guidance of Canon Harford-Battersby. At the first Keswick Convention, more than four hundred persons met under the banner of "All One in Christ Jesus." The meetings have become an annual affair ever since.

From the small community of Keswick in the Lake District of England, the movement quickly spread throughout England, Jamaica, Canada, and the United States. The global spread of Keswick allowed for the spread of the theological emphases of the movement. Unlike other holiness movements with clearly identifiable theological tenets, Keswick tended to be more fluid. It has become known for a much wider theological variety.

Historians will concur that Keswick's theological emphases did not begin in England. The theological emphases had their genesis in the nineteenth century in Philadelphia with Robert and Hannah Smith, born and bred Quakers. In their eighth year of marriage, they were both converted to Christ on the same day. According to Professor Steven Barabas, "The religion they had found seemed to provide perfectly for their future deliverance from sin, but did not seem to give them present deliverance from its power" (*So Great Salvation: The History and Message of the Keswick Convention*, 17). They were caught in the cycle of sinning and repenting as well as making good resolutions and breaking them. They both longed for victory over sin.

As they consulted with older Christians, they were told that the life of sinning and repenting was inevitable because of the weakness of the flesh. Like the apostle Paul, they cried, "What a wretched man I am! Who will rescue me from this body that is subject to death?" (Romans 7:24). They were confident about being justified by faith, but they were unaware of sanctification by faith.

The influence of a young Baptist theological student and a Methodist dressmaker helped Hannah Smith understand what it meant to live victoriously by overcoming the power of sin:

> We had simply discovered the "secret of victory," and knew that we were no longer the "slaves of sin" and therefore forced to yield to its mastery, but that we might, if we would, be made "more than conquerors through him that loved us." (Romans 8:37)

Although neither of the Smiths had theological training, each had an unusual ability to simplify abstract religious truths. They used every possible minute to teach others to live victoriously. Their commitment to the family business and to propagating this message of victory began to impact their health. Their doctor strongly recommended a period of rest. They chose England to get the prescribed rest in 1872.

On their arrival in London, they found that their fame had preceded them. Before long, they were addressing groups on the subject of the higher Christian life. At one of those meetings, the Smiths met Evan Hopkins. Hopkins invited Harford-Battersby to participate and used his influence to launch the first Keswick Convention in 1875. When asked to report on that convention, Harford-Battersby said:

> I had the great privilege of taking part in that ten days of Union Meetings for the promotion of Scriptural holiness, and language fails me to tell of the richness and fullness of the blessing which was poured out upon us during those wondrous gatherings. We were taken out of ourselves; we were led step by step, after deep and close searching of the heart, to such a consecration of ourselves to God, as in the ordinary times of a religious life hardly seemed possible, and we were brought, hundreds of us, clergy and laymen, men and women, to the enjoyment of a peace in trusting Christ for present and future sanctification which exceeded our utmost hopes (*So Great Salvation*, 22).

Harford-Battersby's description of the first convention was also characteristic of future conventions. Conventions were promoted as "union meetings for the promotion of practical holiness." Keswick became the mother of similar conventions in Scotland, Ireland, and other parts of England, and Keswick leaders became the main speakers. With time, as conventions grew across England and around the world, distinctive theological emphases became more evident.

Distinctives

The convention stands for no particular brand of denominational theology. Speakers stressed that the scriptures must be taken seriously. They believed God was speaking through the scriptures. Whereas speakers at other conventions were known for their oratorical skills, theological emphases, and exegetical acumen, Keswick speakers were known for practical holiness. For this reason, convention advertisements included the words "for the promotion of scriptural holiness."

Unlike evangelistic crusades, which are geared to unbelievers, Keswick is unapologetically geared to Christians who see themselves as tired of sin and eager for victory over sin. Some historians even refer to the conventions as spiritual clinics. The convention recognizes that many who attend, especially for the first time, are spiritual causalities.

At a 1905 convention, Dr. A. T. Pearson recalled being invited to address the convention after Rev. E.W. Moore's sermon. Pearson was so convicted by the previous sermon that he acknowledged his brokenness before the congregation. This is how he described his experience:

> So humbling and overwhelming was this conviction, that when called upon to lead in prayer and address the meeting, it was quite involuntary first of all to make a confession and ask others, who likewise had felt conscious of God's direct dealing, to stand before God as those who then and there besought Him to refine us now. In response to that invitation practically the whole tent-full of people rose as one man, and, while prayer was being offered, many joined in an audible "Amen." Not one word of my

proposed address was ever delivered, nor was the subject even indicated.

The prayer was scarcely concluded, when a spirit of penitent confession broke out in every quarter, and I stood there on my feet for about two and a half hours, witnessing the Holy Spirit's wondrous working.

Pearson's 1905 experience has been repeated numerous times in conventions around the world. It is not unusual to see scores of believers weeping after a service. Over the years, thousands have responded to missionary appeals. Hudson Taylor once said that two-thirds of the missionaries in the China Inland Mission were there as a result of the Keswick ministry.

Structure

At the first Keswick Convention in 1875, Harford-Battersby set the opening theme by preaching from Psalm 62:5: "Yes, my soul, find rest in God; my hope comes from him"(NIV).

In *Knowing God Better: The Vision of the Keswick Movement*, Jonathan Lamb said, "There was a particular emphasis on the need and provision for cleansing from sin, and on resting in the sufficiency of Christ." Quite appropriately, the theme for that first convention was "union meetings for the promotion of practical holiness."

That focus on cleansing from sin came to define the start of future conventions around the world. The opening night is best described as a moment of "spiritual diagnosis." On the second day, speakers consider God's provision for sin. Believers are told that the cross of Christ and the presence of the Holy Spirit are the divine solution for every aspect of sin. In addition, attempts to deal with sin by any other means lead to disappointment and failure.

However, it is not enough for the believer to merely know about sin; one must do something about it. That doing something is encouraged on the third day of the convention. This act of full surrender is known as *consecration*. In the Bible, the word *consecration* means "the separation of oneself from things that are unclean, especially anything that would contaminate one's relationship with a perfect God." Consecration also carries the connotation of sanctification, holiness, or purity.

On the fourth day of Keswick conventions, speakers normally emphasize the work of the Holy Spirit in the life of the believer. Traditionally, Keswick tends to be more Calvinistic in its emphasis on the Holy Spirit. For this reason, many believers who subscribe to Arminian theology either avoid that day of Keswick or totally avoid the convention. Both theological camps would agree on the presence of the Holy Spirit in the life of the believer. However, that agreement is not as evident when the role of the Holy Spirit in sanctification is discussed.

Despite these theological differences, Keswick sees the Spirit-filled life as the dominating theme of the convention. Keswick contends that unless believers know what God has to say about the place of the Holy Spirit in their lives—and in the life of the Church—they will find it impossible to live victoriously. Keswick will argue that it is only through the Spirit-filled life that believers can be and do what God wants. How that is accomplished continues to be debatable.

How should one respond when one is filled with the Holy Spirit? The answer to that question is presented on the last day of the convention. The focus is Christian service. The impact of the final day of the convention has had a profound impression on Christian missions around the world. Someone asked one of the Keswick speakers if the convention was a missionary meeting. The speaker answered, "No, but it is a meeting for making missionaries." Literally thousands of Christians have responded to the call to missions on the last night of Keswick.

Hudson Taylor said, "Two-thirds of the missionaries in the China Inland Mission were there as a result of Keswick." Both individual Christians and Christian movements have been positively affected by the ministry of Keswick.

All One in Christ Jesus

Over the main entrance to the large tent in which the meetings are held in Keswick, and also over the platform, is a large sign: "All One in Christ Jesus." When first used in Galatians 3:28, the apostle Paul was emphasizing the oneness believers experience when the Holy Spirit brings them into the church. The distinguishing marks of ethnicity, status, and gender were subordinated to the primacy of oneness in Jesus Christ. That theme is still considered the fundamental platform of all Keswick conventions.

A Keswick convention is a remarkable illustration of that truth. The unity of the Spirit that prevails at conventions is one of its most impressive features. It is one of those rare, if not unique, occasions when members of the clergy sit with their congregants to be able to learn together. It is not unusual to witness missionaries, members of the clergy, members of the organizing committee, and regular attendees together at the altar in tears, responding together, at the end of a sermon.

This spirit of authentic ecumenism often reduces the spirit of rivalry that is evident in many Christian communities. Many churches continue to benefit from pulpit exchanges as an overflow of the spirit of unity generated at Keswick events. Opportunities for united choirs and musicians enable many to hear the voices of fellow believers they would never have heard were it not for Keswick.

Even denominational gatherings are known for controversial preaching. However, that cannot be said of Keswick preachers. Preachers respect the focus of the convention and avoid issues that would divide believers. Interestingly, because of the unity of spirit that prevails at conventions, Keswick has never been found to cause divisions in churches. As worshippers benefit from the ministry of Keswick, they return to their churches renewed to make a difference—rather than inspired to worship elsewhere.

It is obvious that the Keswick movement is an unusual movement of the Holy Spirit. Many biographies have been written on speakers and many histories on the movement, and the consensus is clear.

This movement is raised by God to challenge His people to a path of victorious Christian living.

In South Florida, we sing Francis Bottome's nineteenth-century hymn "Full Salvation" at each service. We realize how privileged we are to be a part of a movement that promotes full salvation in Christ around the world.

Who Is Dr. David Corbin?

The word *diverse* aptly describes Dr. David Corbin. He was born in Trinidad to parents with Barbadian and Vincentian roots. In 1973, he married a Jamaican, and they have adult children who are married to persons of Colombian and Italian backgrounds. Diversity is also reflected in his academic pursuits. He pursued undergraduate studies in the Caribbean and advanced studies in America. His bivocational roles as professor and pastor seem compatible with David's life of diversity and prepared him well for his current pasttime as president of the Caribbean Graduate School of Theology.

Chapter 3

Keswick: A Family Affair
Launa Corbin

When David Corbin migrated to Jamaica in 1971, he had never heard of Keswick. That story changed within months, firstly, because he was attending a Bible college that played a vital role in Kingston Keswick. The other reason was because his best friend, who later became his wife, had been influenced by Keswick in her hometown of Mandeville.

Launa McTaggart was already pursuing theological studies when David arrived on the campus of Jamaica Theological Seminary from Trinidad and Tobago. Her quest to earn an undergraduate degree in theological studies resulted from the impact of Mandeville Keswick on her life. Although Keswick had been in Mandeville since 1900, she knew nothing of the movement prior to 1965. She did not know that hundreds of Christians from all around Jamaica and overseas gathered annually for an entire week of deeper-life services.

Something happened in 1965 that changed her ignorance to interest. Someone she knew in high school became a Christian and began working at a local bank. When Launa joined the bank staff, she reconnected with her old friend. The lifestyle difference was obvious; her friend Colleen Scarlett was converted, and among her new interests was attending Keswick.

Launa's surprise with Colleen's transformation quickly changed to interest in Colleen's transformation. Weeks of inquiry resulted in an invitation to attend one night of the annual event called Keswick. God used the lusty congregational singing, the aura of worship, and the powerful preaching to reinforce a quest for something spiritual. In her own words, Launa admitted, "That night I was miserable. I went home bewildered."

That befuddled feeling continued the following day. The climax came when my colleague introduced me to an American missionary at a local Bible college. I tried to explain my disorientation. Shortly after, I learned that I was experiencing a deep conviction of the Holy Spirit. That conviction ceased when I gave my life to Jesus and was marvelously converted. Now, some fifty years later, I am convinced God used Keswick in the conviction and initial nurturing process of my conversion.

During my fledging faith, God again used Keswick ministry through speakers like Stephen Olford and Ian Barclay to challenge me to a deeper walk with Christ. During a Friday evening service, I responded to a call for Christian service. My response culminated in my application to pursue theological studies at the Jamaica Theological Seminary.

To say I was thrilled would be to put it mildly. My college was actively involved in another Keswick convention, which was launched six years before I arrived. Students were expected to attend morning Bible studies, and many of us opted to attend the evening services. Fortunately, my summer vacations in Mandeville coincided with Keswick, allowing me to benefit from Keswick both in Kingston and Mandeville.

When David arrived in Kingston from Trinidad, his interest in Keswick furthered heightened my interest. Other than seeing Christians from other churches working together at summer camps, he had no point of reference to appreciate Keswick. He was fascinated with the music, the ecumenism, and the preaching from vintage preachers like Skevington Wood and J. Sidlow Baxter.

Like a sponge, David absorbed as much as he could about Keswick during his two years of study in Jamaica. Following our marriage in 1973, we traveled to Trinidad where he assumed leadership in high school student ministry. That year, Keswick ministry began in Trinidad with Dr. Stephen Olford. Although not involved in planning the first convention, David's interest was evident.

By 1976, he was spearheading a second convention in the nation's capital, Port of Spain. We returned to Jamaica after two years in leadership, and David pursued further studies. Because of his interest and experience from the Trinidad convention, David was invited to serve on the planning committee of Kingston Keswick for twelve years before we migrated to the United States.

During that twelve-year stint, David was invited to address conventions in different parts of Jamaica. In 1986, he returned to Trinidad as the keynote speaker for the tenth anniversary of the convention. He also served as the inaugural chairman. In one of his experiences in Barbados, he shared the pulpit with Dr. Paul Rees in the evening of his ministry. They were introduced as the youngest and oldest speakers at the Barbados convention.

At one of the Barbados conventions, David shared the pulpit with Dr. Erwin Lutzer from Moody Church. That contact was critical in that it was used by God to confirm David's recommission to ministry. Later opportunities to minister in Chicago at the historic Moody Church came out of that contact at Barbados Keswick.

David resigned as secretary of Kingston Keswick when we migrated to the United States in 1991. Other than a few opportunities to address Keswick overseas conventions during our graduate studies in the Midwest, our contact with Keswick was minimal until we moved to South Florida in 1999. While in South Florida, we never envisaged reconnecting with Dr. Gerry Gallimore, with whom David served for many years on the Kingston Keswick Council. Along with other local pastors who were familiar with Keswick in Jamaica, a prayer group emerged with the possibility of launching a convention in South Florida.

We never imagined that David's involvement as secretary of this fledging convention would result in our most involved season with Keswick. Consistent with my experience and training in catering, David and I offered to host council breakfast meetings. Our offer provided a stable venue for the meetings and breakfast, an additional incentive to attend council meetings.

Another opportunity presented itself in 2007: hosting the breakfast for leaders on the Saturday morning of the convention weekend. We find it particularly gratifying to see the growth in attendance and to know that God used our availability to accomplish so many things through Keswick ministry.

For almost fifty years, some of our most meaningful friendships have developed through Keswick. Invitations to preach, cater, counsel, and participate at various levels of ministry were triggered by Keswick contacts. And, just at the time we are preparing to allow younger leaders to assume leadership, we are preparing to attend the first Keswick International Consultation in England.

Sometimes we wonder what our ministry would have been like without Keswick. What a thrill our Keswick experience has been to observe so many evangelical Christians crossing denominational boundaries to experience the joy of oneness in Jesus Christ.

As we face the challenges of ministering to believers in this postmodern era, we know Keswick will need to be more creative in its approach to ministry. However, we pray that her mission to bring believers into a deeper life will never die.

Who Is Launa Corbin?

Launa Corbin refers to herself as a sample of God's grace. She believes the circumstances surrounding her birth in Jamaica—and the limited opportunities expected—should have predicted a life of misfortune. But God had other plans. With certification in catering, a graduate degree in counseling, seven grandchildren, three adult children, and more than forty-four years of marriage, Launa says, "I am blessed. I am a sample of God's grace."

Chapter 4

Keswick Convention and Spiritual Growth
Richard Heron

Introduction

The Keswick Convention as a movement is an outgrowth of the Higher Life Movement, which is committed to fostering Christian holiness in England. This began in 1875 at a time when there was renewed interest in sanctification by Methodists and among other Christians outside the Wesleyan tradition. Facing the threat of liberal forces, faithful Christians developed a profound hunger for a deeper knowledge and experience of God. At a time when "destructive forces were wreaking havoc in the soul of the great denominations" by way of modernism, a new movement in pursuit of holiness was emerging among many Christians in England, the United States, and Europe. In 142 years, this movement has grown to become international as Christians long for a deeper walk with God and the experience of practical holiness worldwide.

"Spiritual Formation" as practiced by the Dallas Theological Seminary is "the process by which God forms the character of Christ in believers by the Holy Spirit ... This process involves the transformation of the whole person in desires, thoughts, behaviors, and styles of relating to God and others. Such life change is manifest in a growing love for God and others—dying to self and living for Christ." This is not the same as that practiced by the fledging

Emerging Church, New Age Movement, Eastern Mysticism, and other non-Christian religions. They use extra-biblical functions such as contemplative prayer, meditation, silence, and other mind-emptying practices to enter into "union with God, the Absolute Being."

Spiritual Formation, as used here, is not the result of self-effort. It is produced by the infilling of the Holy Spirit continuing the conversion experience into the personal enjoyment of the abundant life promised by Christ (John 10:10). Biblically, Spiritual Formation is the believer becoming "conformed to the image of His Son" (Romans 8:29). This is the redemptive purpose. Death to self, expressed in total surrender to God and nonconformity to the world as well as the further choice of being "transformed by the renewing of the mind," provide the proper attitude that fosters Spiritual Formation (Romans 12:1–2). This is the required process.

Discipleship is the enabling environment in which the nurturing necessary for growth and development occurs. The goal of this growth and development is the outward expression of the character of Christ in the life of believers. To that end, Paul in Galatians 4:19 depicts himself as a loving mother going through the pangs of childbearing until their conduct is so transformed that it is reflecting the image of Christ.

> And we all, who with unveiled faces contemplate the Lord's glory, are being transformed into his image with ever-increasing glory, which comes from the Lord, who is the Spirit. (2 Corinthians 3:18)

This is the disciple-making product. Just as an embryo must grow into a fully developed child, so the character of Christ in the believer must be allowed its full expression. This comes from obeying the injunction to "work out your salvation" (Philippians 2:12–13). The good news here is that it is God at work within believers who provides the enabling to think, feel, and do what pleases God just as Christ pleased the Father in all things (John 8:29). Disciples are believers who allow Christ's teachings to reform their behavior patterns to become like Christ.

To the Thessalonians, Paul was a nursing mother tenderly caring for her own children and a superintending father urging, encouraging, and pleading that they live worthy of God as "kingdom" people (1 Thessalonians 2:7–8; 11–12). Keswick speakers seek to fill the shoes of the apostle Paul as they minister to Christians who desire to move toward maturity. Their commitment to the Gospel and their understanding of the redemptive purpose, the required process, and the disciple-making product position them as facilitators who passionately expound God's Word, faithfully present Jesus Christ as Lord, and always give opportunity for the Holy Spirit to lead listeners to apply God's Word to their situations.

The Original Intent of the Keswick Movement

The original intent of the Keswick Movement was to facilitate the experience of entire sanctification as taught in the scriptures:

> Make every effort to live in peace with everyone and to be holy; without holiness no one will see the Lord. (Hebrews 12:14)

> May God himself, the God of peace, sanctify you through and through. May your whole spirit, soul and body be kept blameless at the coming of our Lord Jesus Christ. (1 Thessalonians 5:23)

This is the initial step as well as the continual process of spiritual formation. As a result, the early speakers were chosen from among men who themselves had come to discover and experience the fullness of blessings of life in Christ through the work of the Holy Spirit. To the pioneers, this was so important that although the "holiness teaching" was first promoted by John Wesley, the founder of Methodism, they did not feel free to invite Methodist ministers as speakers until much later when they were convinced that they too were emphasizing positional as well as experiential or practical sanctification, and were committed to assisting in facilitating this movement.

The Standard Format Unique to Keswick

At age twenty-four, I was both married and appointed to my first pastorate. I was a young Christian, but I felt an insatiable hunger for a deeper knowledge of God and the experience of the fullness of the life of Christ and the Holy Spirit. My wife, Myrtle, was introduced to Keswick as a student at Jamaica Bible College (now Regent College) in Mandeville.

Mandeville Keswick happened to host the first Keswick convention outside of Keswick, England. Jamaica Bible College provided housing for Christians who came from out of town, forming what was known as the "house party." My quest for more of God, my wife's prior involvement, and close proximity to home made it easy to attend. This was providential since I was longing for sound teaching, wonderful fellowship, and the opportunity to apply God's Word on the stop in the presence of other seeking Christians.

I soon discovered that each speaker followed a format at every convention. This was carefully designed to lead believers step-by-step to experience "fullness of power for life and service."

The focus of the opening session is the tragic reality of sin. Scripture is used to expose the various aspects of sin such as the penalty, the power, the presence, and the principle. Without any doubt, this is the most uncomfortable session. Hearers are made to deal with "the exceedingly sinfulness of sin." Sin that is at work in our mortal bodies must not have dominion over us!

One teaching about sin relates to Samson (Judges 16:21–22). The Lord departs, and the mighty Samson is easily bound, blinded, and made to grind at the mill of the enemy. This is a sad picture of the ravages of sin. God's champion does not know that God—the source of his strength—had departed from him. He is asleep in the lap of his paramour. The picture eventually gets worse, demonstrating that sin binds, blinds, and grinds, making the uncommitted slaves to God's enemy. Again, there is good news. As Samson's hair began to grow, his consecration was renewed. His strength returned, and God used him to do greater work for God and His people. This is what the Keswick Movement is about: fostering victorious living.

The second session is usually more comforting since it is a declaration that cleansing and renewal is possible through Christ who lives in us. Here we learned the secret of "keeping short accounts with God." That means that we must repent and forsake sin in our lives. God is faithful and just to forgive sin that is confessed. In John 21, Peter wept bitterly when he realized that—despite his boasting about dying with Christ—he had miserably denied Him (Luke 22:60–62). After His resurrection, Christ helped him to confess his failure, and he was reinstated as a follower of Christ.

The third session deals with the practical response of full surrender to God who has given His all and demands our all.

At one convention, it was pointed out that the believer's commitment to God should be patterned after Christ's commitment as the quintessential servant as modeled by the Hebrew servant of Exodus 21. There, as in Hebrews 10:5–9, commitment is personal, total, and continual. Out of love for his master, his wife, and his children, he elects to serve for the rest of his life.

Christ's commitment involves His ear and His body—not merely for a lifetime but forever. Like Jesus, the believer's submission that is pleasing to God is sacrificial. "And by that will, we have been made holy through the sacrifice of the body of Jesus Christ once for all" (Hebrews 10:10).

Romans 12:1–2 also supports the need for sacrificial submission:

> Therefore... offer your bodies as a living sacrifice, holy and pleasing to God—this is your true and proper worship. ...Then you will be able to test and approve what God's will is—his good, pleasing and perfect will.

A lesson learned is that God can't do anything with us without us; we must make room for God who has acted for us to act in us and through us.

During the fourth session, the person and work of the Holy Spirit is shown as the means by which believers who have been sanctified are being sanctified. "For by one sacrifice he has made perfect forever those who are being made holy" (Hebrews 10:14).

We do the imputing, and He does the imparting. One Keswick speaker—in teaching about the role of the Holy Spirit in the life of believers—commented about the eleven into whose nostrils he individually breathed the Holy Spirit (John 20:22). He instructed them to wait for the promise of the Father to empower them to become witnesses (Acts 1:4–8). According Acts 15:8–9, the presence of the Holy Spirit also "purified their hearts by faith."

In the final session, the emphasis is on missions. Believers are challenged to engage in unconditional service in the kingdom. The Holy Spirit is the Spirit of missions, so He empowers us to live sanctified lives and bear witness of Him. Jesus Christ is the river of living waters, and believers are the channels through which His living-giving presence flows to the world (John 7:38–39). Speakers often reminded us that Christ Church is the only institution that doesn't exist for her personal benefit; it is primarily meant to be evangelistic. Our mission is to make disciples of all nations; our mission field is where we live, work, and do business.

Although the Gospel of Christ is invariably taught, this is not an Evangelistic conference. Similarly, although the teaching is always centered on the Bible, it is not a Bible conference. Also, although in order to elicit a response to greater service, the needs of the world are featured, yet this is not a missionary conference. It is primarily a deeper life conference where God's people expect to be quickened with fresh power appropriated, discovery of our inheritance in Christ, and the rest that comes from full surrender to Christ and the Holy Spirit in the form of the rivers of living waters from Christ.

This standard format was helpful to me so that, at the end, I was not left with another "shot in the arm" but with a path to use in my daily walk with God. With this sequence as my daily routine, I find myself calling a spade a spade. I call sin a sin, and I know I must appropriate the cleansing from Christ's blood and His Word.

I strive to fully surrender my all to all that Christ has given me. The biggest struggle is to walk along this path of holiness in unbroken fellowship with the Holy Spirit, but I know I must because that's the only way to be an overcomer.

Daily Bible Reading

Another component of this format is the daily midmorning Bible reading led by the Keswick speaker. Speakers I cannot forget include Dr. Stephen F. Olford, Dr. Alan Redpath, Vicar J. Alec Motyer, Bishop Festo Kivengere, Dr. Wingrove Taylor, Major W. Ian Thomas, Dr. J. Sidlow Baxter, Dr. Samuel G. Hines, Dr. Herbert Swaby, Dr. James Earl Massey, Pastor Peter M. Lloyd, and Dr. Robert A. Kennedy.

The following exposition of Galatians 2:20 by Dr. Stephen Olford is an example of a Bible reading session. The apostle Paul began by explaining the context of the text in which he is defending the truth of the Gospel. The central truth of the Gospel is the cross of Christ and that the crucified life is to be embraced if one is to become an overcomer. In verse 16, Paul reiterates that "a person is justified not by the works of the law but by faith in Jesus Christ."

Peter, Barnabas, and other so-called leaders were undercutting the message of the Gospel of the grace of God. By refusing to eat with Gentile believers in the presence of Jewish believers, they were deceitfully inferring that you have to become a Jew through the works of the law in order to become a Christian. That was not the first time Peter was "dodging the cross." He also rebuked the Lord Jesus when He announced the necessity of His death.

Peter's refusal to accept the way of the cross eventually led to the shameful denial of his Lord—even after boasting that he would lay down his life for Jesus's sake (John 13:37; see Matthew 26:30–35; Mark 14:30–31; Luke 22:31–34). The immediate context of this verse teaches that the death Christ died is the death we must die. The Master told the disciples,

> Whoever wants to be my disciple must deny themselves and take up their cross and follow me. For whoever wants to save their life will lose it, but whoever loses their life for me will find it. What good will it be for someone to gain the whole world, yet forfeit their soul? Or what can anyone give in exchange for their soul? (Matthew 16:24–26)

Dr. Olford explained the content of this verse as the great doctrine of justification by grace through faith mentioned five times in Galatians 2:17–21. Quoting Martin Luther, he states:

> This is the truth of the Gospel. It is also the principal article of all Christian doctrine, wherein the knowledge of all godliness consists. Most necessary it is, therefore, that we should know this article well, teach it unto others, and beat it into their heads continually.

To summarize what Paul teaches in this passage, he quotes Canon John R. W. Stott:

> Jesus Christ came into the world to live and to die. In His life His obedience to the law was perfect. In His death He suffered for our disobedience. On earth he lived the only life of sinless obedience to the law which has ever been lived. On the cross He dies for our law breaking since the penalty for disobedience to the law was death. All that is required of us to be justified, therefore, is to acknowledge our sin and helplessness, to repent of our years of self-assertion

and self-righteousness, and to put our whole trust and confidence in Jesus Christ to save us.

"Faith in Jesus Christ" is not only an intellectual conviction; it is a personal commitment. The expression in the middle of Galatians 2:16 is "we have believed in Christ Jesus." It is an act of committal. It is not just assenting to the fact that Jesus lived and died; it is running to Him for refuge and calling on Him for mercy.

Justification is not only a legal fact in which we are declared righteous by a holy God; it is also a transforming experience through a living identification with Christ (Galatians 2:17). By union with Christ, we are radically transformed. We can no longer go back to our old lives because in Christ we are "a new creation" (2 Corinthians 5:17).

Having explained the context of the verse that emphasizes the cross of Christ as central to the content of the text that enunciates the great doctrine of justification not by works of the law but through faith in Jesus Christ, Dr. Olford introduced what he now sees as the challenge of this verse:

> I have been crucified with Christ and I no longer live, but Christ lives in me. The life I now live in the body, I live by faith in the Son of God, who loved me and gave himself for me. (Galatians 2:20)

This is one of Paul's understandings of the Gospel of the grace of God. It is the Gospel of the extinguished life: "I have been crucified with Christ" (Galatians 2:20). Believing in Christ means dying to the law since when Christ died, He died under the law's penalty. In so doing, he satisfied the law's demands. As Paul says, the law has no hold on one who is dead. But being crucified also means death to self. Through the death of Christ, the dominating control of the fallen nature has been broken. If we do not understand this, then we are missing something very important. The extinguished life means death to self and sin.

In *The Christ-Life for the Self-Life* (addresses delivered mainly at Carnegie Hall in New York during an ever-memorable week), F. B. Meyer writes:

> The curse of the Christian and of the world is that self is our pivot; it is because Satan made self his pivot that he became a devil. Take heaven from its center in God, and try to center it in self, and you transform heaven into hell.... The philosophy of the Bible is to do away with self and to make Christ all in all. When dealing with a drunkard, I am inclined to say to him, "Be a man." What a fool I am! I am trying to cast out the evil of drink by the evil of self-esteem. If I want to save a man, I must cast out the spirit of self and substitute the Lord Jesus Christ. Alpha, Omega, all in all! But, how? This epistle to the Galatians is my battle-axe. Luther used it for justification, but I think it is for sanctification. How? By the cross, and by the cross as presented in the epistle to the Galatians! (see Galatians 2:20, Galatians 3:1; Galatians 5:24; Galatians 6:14)

The apostle says, "Jesus Christ ... gave Himself for our sins, that He might deliver us from his present evil world, according to the will of God and our Father" (Galatians 1:4). He considers the cross in its aspect toward sanctification. He says, "He delivered us from this present evil world." In Romans, we have the cross for justification and the putting away of sin. In Galatians, we have sanctification and the cross standing between me and my past, between me and the world, and between me and myself. In Galatians 2:20, we have the Gospel of the extinguished life.

It is also the Gospel of the relinquished life:

> I have been crucified with Christ and I no longer live, but Christ lives in me. The life I now live in the

body, I live by faith in the Son of God, who loved me and gave himself for me. (Galatians 2:20)

We no longer lead self-centered lives; we lead Christ-centered ones. By the ministry of the Holy Spirit, the Lord Jesus lives out His life in us day by day as we maintain total dependence on Him. The apostle says the same thing in his letter to the Romans:

> Do not offer any part of yourself to sin as an instrument of wickedness, but rather offer yourselves to God as those who have been brought from death to life; and offer every part of yourself to him as an instrument of righteousness. (Romans 6:13)

We do not relinquish ourselves to an enemy; we present ourselves as a bride to the bridegroom who has wooed and won us in love.

As a pastor, I have had the privilege of marrying couples countless times. As the two stand before me, I say to the bride, "Will you have this man to be your lawful wedded husband?" She answers in two words, "I will," and they are joined for life. That is the kind of presentation we are thinking of when we speak of the relinquished life. We are saying, in effect, "Lord, I am married to You, being alive from the dead, to bring forth fruit unto God. Lord, from now on, my language and life are two words: "I will." Every day we must repeat that once-and-for-all interaction: "I am wholly Yours, Lord. Use me for Your glory."

Once again, it is the Gospel of the distinguished life:

> The life I now live in the body, I live by faith in the Son of God, who loved me and gave himself for me. (Galatians 2:20)

The phrase "faith in the Son of God" is loaded with rich meaning. Because of our union with Christ crucified and risen, we are privileged to "participate in the divine nature" (2 Peter 1:4). We actually share the distinguished life with the Son of God.

Two aspects of this distinctive life are spelled out for us. As the Son of God, our Lord in His perfect humanity chose to live a dependent life. He lived by faith (see John 5:19, John 5:30; John 6:57; John 8:28; and John 14:10). We also must live by faith (Romans 1:17; Hebrews 11:6).

The other distinctive is that the Son of God lived a devoted life. He "gave Himself for [us]" (Galatians 2:20). That takes in the entire sweep of His life, service, and even death in response to the will of His Father.

In similar fashion, we are called to the high and holy distinction of yielding ourselves to God as living sacrifices so that we might "be able to test and approve what God's will is—his good, pleasing, and perfect will" (Romans 12:1–2).

Dependence on God and devotion to God are the marks of divine distinction. Such distinctiveness can be detected anywhere and under any circumstances by a watching world. Out of such a life, the streams of living water flow in blessing to others. This is the testimony of God's people throughout the centuries.

Martin Luther experienced this blessing. He was a showpiece of discipline, penance, self-denial, and self-torture. He said, "If ever a man could be saved by monkery, that man was I." He had gone to Rome. It was considered an act of great merit to climb the Scala Sancta, the great sacred stairway, on hands and knees. He toiled upward, seeking that merit that he might win; suddenly, there came to mind the voice from heaven: "The just shall live by faith."

The life at peace with God was not to be attained by this futile, never-ending, ever-defeated effort; it could only be had by casting himself on the love and mercy of God as Jesus Christ has revealed them to men. Peace comes when we give up the struggle the pride of self thinks it can win—but must ever lose—and when we abandon ourselves to the forgiving love of God.

The blessing that flowed from Luther's life changed the face of Europe—and, ultimately, affected the fate of millions. John Wesley's cultured mind was matched only by his spiritual sensitivity, servant attitude, and social concern, but he was a discouraged man when he returned to England from Savannah, Georgia. He had encountered great problems in his attempt to deal with the colonists in the New World. Indeed, the outward and inward battles brought him to doubt his own acceptability before the God he loved and served.

In that frame of mind, he reluctantly went to a meeting where Luther's *Preface to the Epistle to the Romans* was read. During the reading, Wesley's "heart was strangely warmed." He recorded in his journal:

> I felt I did trust in Christ alone for salvation; and an assurance was given to me that He had taken away my sins, even mine, and saved me from "the law of sin and death."

Armed with this message of union with Christ in His death and resurrection, John Wesley embarked on forty years of full-time ministry. So mightily did the Spirit of God use him that revivals blazed in England and America throughout the eighteenth and nineteenth centuries, and the course of history was changed.

In *They Found the Secret*, the beloved former president and chancellor of Wheaton College, Dr. V. Raymond Edman, shared the testimonies of men and women who experienced the blessing of life "in Christ." His purpose "was to show ... how the power of Christ, [which he called] "the indwelling life of Christ," was the source of every believer's spiritual strength."

Dr. Edman felt that evangelicals had largely neglected this theme for many years.

> Put the idea into the mainstream of Christian thought so that all could benefit by entering into a life-transforming relationship with Christ. It is not enough just to know about Christ or to know about what He did for us or even to experience His work in us. What is needed is to experience Him in us as He works out God's inscrutable will.

Here is the testimony of one who discovered the secret of the exchanged life.

The crisis of the deeper life came to John Bunyan as he was walking in the fields.

> "Suddenly," he said, "this sentence fell upon my soul, Thy righteous is in heaven." And me thought with awe, I saw, with the eyes of my soul Jesus Christ at God's right hand ... It was glorious to me to see his exaltation and the worth and prevalence of all his benefits." Ephesians 5:30 became "a sweet word" to him: "For we are members of his body." He could say: "The Lord did also lead me into the mystery of union with the Son of God.... By this also was my faith in him, as my righteousness, the more confirmed in me; for if he and I were one, then his righteousness was mine, his merits mine, his victory also mine. Now I could see myself in heaven and earth at once; in heaven by my Christ, by my head, by my righteousness and life, though on earth by my body or person."

And what were the results of Bunyan's being unchained from his doubts and fears? Among them, he lists grace that could keep him in deepest difficulties, insight into the scriptures, no fear of death, an assurance of his Lord's presence with him, and a fruitful service for the Savior both in the pulpit and in the prison.

Devotional literature is replete with similar testimonies, but the example cited above illustrates the blessing we can know when we understand and appropriate the truth embodied in Galatians 2:20. As God's people, we must be willing to pray and mean:

> Crucified with Christ, my Savior,
> I am dead to sin and shame;
> Now his life rules my behavior —
> To the glory of His Name! Amen.

Such exposition of scripture becomes an invaluable input in the process of Spiritual Formation. In each session, the Word of God is exposed to the magnifying glass of the Holy Spirit, revealing essential truths that are understood in ways that can be applied to daily living.

Books by Keswick Speakers

The influence of the teachings of Keswick continues through the recordings and writings of the speakers. These contain priceless truths the Lord will use to open the eyes of our hearts to the immeasurable greatness of His power. Some of these are Major Ian Thomas's *The Saving Life of Christ* and *The Mystery of Godliness* and *If I Perish, I Perish;* J. Sidlow Baxter's *Our High Calling, His Deeper Work in Us,* and *A New Call to Holiness,* and J. Alec Motyer's *Commentary of Isaiah.*

Hymns

Hymns from the Keswick Praise hymnal continue to be a source of inspiration and contributor to Spiritual Formation. Here is one of the favorites:

Jesus I Am Resting, Resting
(Jean Sophia Pigott, 1845–1882)

Jesus I am resting, resting
In the joy of what Thou art;
I am finding out the greatness
Of Thy loving heart.
Thou hast bid me gaze upon Thee,
And Thy beauty fills my soul,
For, by Thy transforming power,
Thou hast made me whole.
    O how great Thy loving-kindness,
    Vaster, broader than the sea!
O how marvelous Thy goodness,

Lavished all on me!
Yes, I rest in Thee Beloved,
Know what grace and wealth is Thine,
Know Thy certainty of promise
And have made it mine.
Simply trusting Thee, Lord Jesus,
I behold Thee as Thou art,
And Thy love so pure, so changeless,
Satisfies my heart;
Satisfies its deepest longings,
Meets, supplies its every need,
Compasses me round with blessings;
Thine is love indeed!
Ever lift Thy face upon me,
As I work and wait for Thee;
Resting 'neath Thy smile, Lord Jesus,
Earth's dark shadows flee,
Brightness of my Father's glory,
Sunshine of my Father's face,
Keep me ever trusting, resting,
Fill me with Thy grace.

Who Is Richard Heron?

Richard Heron was born and educated in Jamaica. His professional life included years in the life insurance industry, where he became a manager. He served in Christian ministry for more than fifty years. He served as a pastor for thirty-eight years, and as director and president of two mission agencies for twenty-seven years. His key ministry areas are leadership development, local church revitalization, disaster relief, and sustainable development.

Richard has been married to Myrtle for fifty-five years, and he has two grown daughters, three grandchildren, and a host of surrogate children. He was awarded the honorary doctor of divinity degree from the Atlantic College and Theological Seminary for his work in the churches in Haiti.

Chapter 5

Immigration: Bane and Blessing (Implications for South Florida Keswick)
Rev. Dr. Raymond Anglin

Introduction

In 2016, immigration dominated the casual conversation of people on the streets, it was a priority on the agendas of the president of the United States and the Supreme Court, and it was a hot subject for debate in the campaign for the presidency of the United States. The irony of this, however, is that there seem to be a questioning of the fact that the United States has historically been comprised of people from all nations of the world who have migrated to make this country their home. So, everyone here has come directly or indirectly through family descendants, has been born here with family connections, or has come from somewhere else.

With this being stated, it is important to explore whether immigration as a phenomenon has had a negative or positive impact on the country in general and on South Florida in particular. A further matter of concern is how it has impacted South Florida. What is the impact on the church in South Florida? What are the implications for South Florida Keswick? In other words, is it a bane or a blessing?

For the purpose of this discussion, it is necessary to define the concepts being explored:

- Bane: A person or thing that ruins or spoils, a deadly poison.
- Baneful: Destructive, pernicious, or poisonous.[1]
- Blessing: A special favor, mercy or benefit, the blessings of liberty, a favor or gift bestowed by God, thereby bringing happiness.[2]

One understands that any discussion on the issue of immigration will present varying perspectives formed from experiences and knowledge. I invite the reader to approach the subject with an open mind.

Acknowledgement and Not Approval

To begin, we need to note that there has been much attention given to this subject by a variety of sources—be it individual or collective. Some come from primarily objective positions, and others have subjective and self-serving positions.

An October 23, 2014, article by the Center for American Progress highlighted a number of important factors.[3] Immigration has been a constant source of economic vitality and demographic dynamism throughout our nation's history. Immigrants are taxpayers, entrepreneurs, job creators, and consumers.

The article further acknowledged that the foreign-born population in the United States in 2012 consisted of 40.7 million people. Broken down by immigration status, the foreign-born population was composed of 18.6 million naturalized American citizens and 22.1 million noncitizens. Of the noncitizens, approximately 13.3 million

---

[1] Webster's College Dictionary.
[2] Ibid.
[3] Center for American Progress, *The Facts on Immigration Today*, October 23, 2014.

were legal permanent residents, 11.3 million were unauthorized migrants, and 1.9 million were on temporary visas.

Between 2000 and 2012, there was a significant increase in the foreign-born population. There was a 31.2 percent increase, and the immigrant population grew from 31.1 million to 40.8 million people.

The foreign-born share of the population more than doubled since the 1960s, but it was still below its all-time high. The immigrant population was 5.4 percent of the total American population in 1960. By 2012, immigrants made up 13 percent of the total American population. And still, today's share of the immigrant population as a percentage of the total American population remains below its peak in 1890, when 14.8 percent of the American population had migrated to the country.

When immigrants arrive in this country, they immediately begin the process of settling down and putting down roots all across the United States, including South Florida where the climate is tropical and warm. They have a wide range of experiences and diverse educational backgrounds. In 2012, 11.6 percent of immigrants had master's, professional, or doctorate degrees—compared with 10.8 percent of the native-born population. That same year, 69.4 percent of the foreign-born population had attained a high school diploma, GED, or higher, compared with 89.9 percent of the native-born population.

More than half of the foreign-born residents are homeowners. In 2012, 51 percent of immigrant heads of household owned their homes—compared with 66 percent of native-born heads of household. Among immigrants, 65 percent of naturalized citizens owned their own homes in 2012.

By way of emphasis, it must be noted that the statistical data cited above, while it is nationally referenced, does apply to the local states and is evidenced in the local communities and is accurately descriptive of South Florida.

Much of this is acknowledged as being positive. However, there are some equally negative aspects to this phenomenon. Less than one in five immigrants live in poverty, and they are more likely to use social services. In 2012, 19.1 percent of immigrants lived in poverty, while 15.4 percent of the native-born population lived in poverty. Of the foreign-born, the largest groups living in poverty were the 3.2 million who emigrated from Mexico and the 1.4 million people who emigrated from either South or East Asia. Despite this, studies have consistently shown that immigrants use social programs such as Medicaid and Supplemental Security Income at similar rates to native households.

It has already been noted that immigrants include many who are undocumented (not having legal documents for residence). However, this undocumented population has remained relatively stable. Six states are home to the majority of this population; 22 percent lives in California, 15 percent lives in Texas, 8 percent lives in Florida, 7 percent lives in New York, 4 percent lives in Illinois, and 4 percent lives in New Jersey.

The 8 percent of undocumented immigrants—when added to the vast number of legal immigrants—results in a rather substantial group of immigrants living in Florida in general and in South Florida in particular. This impacts all aspects of our shared life: economic, social, educational, health, political, and religious. For some people, this experience is baneful, and for others, it is a blessing.

While it is definitely not the author's intention to give a general approval to the facts stated above, it is the intention to have them acknowledged. Immigration plays an important role and immigrants contribute to this nation and its states. These facts should not get lost in conversations and debates. Except for the small minority of Americans who are descendants of native Americans, the overwhelming majority of American citizens and residents are immigrants or descendants of immigrants.

Acceptance and Not Accommodation

Having hopefully argued for the place and role of immigrants in South Florida, it would seem logical to move to looking at their relationship with their communities. How are immigrants treated?

As an immigrant, the writer is able to identify fully with this and will be very careful not to be overly subjective.

In the Hebrew scriptures, the term used closest to the immigrant is the word *sojourner*, which refers to a person living in mutually responsible association with a community or place—not inherently his or her own. This word is also translated as *stranger* or *alien:*

- "Do not mistreat an alien or oppress him, for you were aliens in Egypt. (Exodus 22:21)
- Do not oppress an alien; you yourselves know how it feels to be aliens, because you were aliens in Egypt. (Exodus 23:9)

There were many other references to the sojourner, the stranger, or the alien. They all refer to the person who occupied a position between that of the native-born and the foreigner. He has come among a people distinct from him and thus lacks the protection and benefits ordinarily provided by kin and birthplace. His status and privileges derive from the bond of hospitality, in which the guest is inviolable.

These references hopefully remind us of the fundamental fact that we belong—individually and collectively—to the Creator. Therefore, for the person of faith, that reality is experienced in a relationship with God. That relationship was established through the covenant of the Old Testament and reinterpreted and completed in the New Testament in Jesus Christ.

The almighty Father was always concerned about the individual. He made sure the immigrant was cared for—no matter the context of living—and this was clearly the case throughout Old Testament history. The immigrant was to be accepted and not merely accommodated. The existential reality is that the immigrant also experiences a need for the spiritual, a need for God before whom all creatures appear naked and from whom nothing can be hidden. The philosopher, Soren Kierkegaard spoke of the "deep moments of the soul."

When immigrants leave their native lands and arrive here, they bring much of their own culture with them, including the need for religious expression. In South Florida, there are a variety of churches and places of worship in the communities. Some of these are very well established and traditional, and others are more recently established or new.

The desire of many immigrants has been to find the church that is similar to that to which they have been accustomed and consistent with their faith and belief construct. Unfortunately, this has not been the case for many. They become preoccupied with survival needs, and in many instances, they fall by the wayside, making them "objects for evangelism."

Other immigrants visit their neighborhood churches in pursuit of fellowship—only to feel unwelcomed or merely accommodated because of the skin pigmentation or class stratification.

What the immigrant needs is that place where he or she is welcomed and accepted for who they are and not merely accommodated. That is hypocrisy and pretense.

Assimilation and Not Alienation

Throughout the life and ministry of Jesus, he was always seen ministering among the crowds, but he maintained consistent concern for the individuals he encountered. All four Gospels record these encounters, demonstrating how he was "moved with compassion," which resulted in action to cure the leper, heal the sick, feed the hungry, give sight to the blind, and raise the dead. Then he commissioned His disciples:

> Go and make disciples of all nations, baptizing them in the name of the Father and the Son and the Holy Spirit, and teaching them to obey everything I have commanded you. And surely I am with you always, to the end of the age. (Matthew 28:19–20)

After being commissioned, the core group was empowered to continue the ministry, beginning in Jerusalem, Judea, Samaria, and to the utmost ends of the earth.

During this period, the good news of the Gospel was proclaimed, the church expanded, and converts were baptized, nurtured, and assimilated into the fellowship of the church. There was constant appeal for unity, and the apostle Paul was the primary proponent for this among the churches.

This was the burning desire of pastors from the Caribbean who had come to the United States, themselves being immigrants, to provide a context for this unity among the churches in South Florida to be experienced and visibly expressed. This led to the birth of South Florida Keswick. This fledgling movement has brought congregations comprised primarily of immigrants together annually, since 2002, to celebrate their unity in Christ:

> There is neither Jew nor Greek, slave nor free, male nor female, for you are all one in Christ Jesus. (Galatians 3:28)

And this has been the theme of Keswick: "All one is Christ Jesus."

As churches come together each year and celebrate with inspiring music, joyful singing, power-filled exegetical preaching, and embracing and enriching fellowship, South Florida Keswick becomes "a place of belonging" for immigrants, sojourners, aliens, and strangers.

In the celebrations, immigrant Christians are challenged to:

- remember their *primary ethnicity*—the family in which they were born, their ancestors and descendants;
- recall their *personal history*—the personal stories ought to be recalled and transmitted from generation to generation; and
- revel in their *peculiar community*—celebrate their baptism, celebrate in fellowship, and cooperate in ministry within and mission without.

The challenge for South Florida Keswick is to ensure that as the churches gather each year, the context is created for these to occur.

And as they are refueled, reignited, and recharged spiritually, they commit to return to their individual congregations and continue engagement in ministry that seeks always to assimilate and not alienate immigrant brothers and sisters. They are urged to go beyond the compartments of self-comfort and into the complexities that are integral to the lives of our immigrant members and their communities.

Who Is Raymond Anglin?

Raymond Anglin has served as pastor, administrator, professor, and consultant in the Jamaica Baptist Union and the Presbyterian Church in Georgia and Florida. Raymond is a founding member of South Florida Keswick and received his undergraduate degree from the United Theological College of the West Indies (Jamaica) and graduate degrees from Pittsburgh Theological Seminary. He retired from active pastoring but continues to serve on several committees. Raymond and his wife, Pauline, have been married for forty-six years and have four sons and eight grandchildren.

Chapter 6

The Impact of Music on the Keswick Convention
Reginald G. Smith

Introduction

Inasmuch as the Keswick Convention has become an international ministry with a mission focus on deeper Christian spiritual life, the purpose of this chapter was originally intended to lift up the impact of music on the South Florida Keswick Convention. However, it seemed reasonable to try to discover how the parent convention in Keswick England, in 1875, factored music into its projection and practice of ministry. To an island-based cleric, that discovery promised to have a special opportunity since Keswick music just had to be Eurocentric in character. In case that sounds like a novel expectation, let it be understood that, by colonial inheritance, music in the bygone days of the British Empire was and has been Eurocentric, notwithstanding the introduction of other musical genres in the former British colonies.

It seemed like sought-after information was not forthcoming until I was wonderfully favored. Rev. Phillip Sowerbutts, vicar of Castle Church in Stafford, England, gave me a chapter excerpt entitled "Full Salvation: Keswick and Worship," which is part of a larger work entitled "Transforming Keswick." That chapter has been summarized just before the "South Florida Keswick" section and the conclusion.

The Historical Role of Music in Worship

One of the earliest known definitions of music familiar to Jamaican music students came from their instructors:

> Music is a language expressing feelings and ideas and is governed by the first letters of the alphabet namely, A, B, C, D, E, F, G. Music is even believed to be of heavenly origin. It is a gift from God and has the potential to give lift to one's thoughts in order to inspire and elevate the soul.[4]

The Old Testament is laced with references to music. Jubal was "the father of all such as handle the harp and organ (Genesis 4:21). He was the inventor of wind and stringed instruments. Jubilee is derived from the name Jubal.

Laban reprimanded Jacob for stealing away secretly when Laban had been aware of Jacob's plans: "I might have sent thee away with mirth and with songs and with tambourines and with lyres" (Genesis 31:27).

Old Testament worship is primarily focused on presenting Jehovah as Sovereign God, while the message of New Testament music and worship requires a solid foundation on the Word of God for teaching and building up the body of Christ. (Acts 2:42, Colossians 3:16–17). Here are some examples of the impact and relevance of music in Old Testament narratives:

---

[4] White, Ellen G., *Music: Its Role, Qualities, and Influence: A Compilation of Materials Assembled for Study by the 1972 Task Force on Philosophy of Music*, Silver Spring, Maryland, 1972, 2.

- Shortly after the Exodus, more than one million people sang a victory song. (Exodus 15:11)
- Miriam and several women celebrated with timbrels and dances. "Sing to the Lord for He is highly exalted. Both horse and driver he has hurled into the sea. (Exodus 15:11)
- Moses instructed Israel by way of song before he died. (Exodus 15:21)
- Priests bearing ram horns and trumpets marched before the ark. (Joshua 6:4)
- The Song of Deborah which celebrated a military victory. (Judges 5:1-3)
- Jephthah's daughter used instruments of music in returning to greet her father. (Judges 11:34)
- David upon returning from the Philistine slaughter was greeted by singing and dancing and with instruments of music. (1 Samuel 18:6)
- David played the harp to comfort Saul. (1 Samuel 18:10)
- David was known to employ musicians to serve in divine services, and he even prophesied by means of hymns. (1 Chronicles 25:1-3)
- Instrumental music was commanded by God. (2 Chronicles 29:25)
- There was a staff of professional musicians performing in the temple and the palace. (1 Chronicles 14:22)
- Four thousand men praised God with "instruments of music of the Lord." (2 Chronicles 7:6)
- At the dedication of Solomon's temple, cymbals, psalteries, harps, and trumpets accompanied praise. (2 Chronicles 5:12-14)
- He even provided housing for a paid choir. (2 Chronicles 29:25-29)

George L. Faull, in an article entitled "Music in the Old Testament: A Brief History of Music to David," speculates that John Calvin must have been solidly inspired when he characterized the Psalms as "an anatomy of all parts of the soul." (http://www.summit1.org).

Obviously, Old Testament leaders were convinced about the need for music in praise and worship. Music was a language for expressing deep joy, happiness, and devotion.

Ellen G. White holds that something sacred in the human voice surpasses any other musical instrument and is one of God's gifts to men and women for use in glorifying Him. Music is also conceptualized as a cultural expression that should deepen and provide greater texture to our experience of the world.[5]

The power of song is exemplified as the Israelites were cheered by music and songs during the biblical Exodus. It is assumed that their singing must have fixed words in their memory, awakened sympathy, and promoted harmony in action, thereby banishing gloom. As a weapon against discouragement, music can impart power and gladness to longing souls. As an act of worship, it is believed that music must have encouraged the setting of the words of the law to music.[6]

The human voice does not produce beautiful music through loud singing. Some singers believe that the louder they sing, the more music they make, but it ought to be appreciated that noise is not music. God is not pleased with discord. Rather, it is harmonious music that glorifies God and achieves singing with the spirit and with understanding. The Holy Spirit does not reveal Himself in bedlam, and shouting is not evidence of authentic Christian spirituality. Singing with the spirit and with the understanding impress spiritual truths upon the heart.

This question may be appropriately raised. What is music in the light of worshipping God? According to Michael Joseph Brown, in Matthew 6:1, Jesus is saying that if the intention behind our singing is to be seen by the human audience, then we are engaging in theater,

---

[5] Abingdon, James, *Readings in African American Church Music and Worship*, volume 2, GIA Publications, Inc. Chicago, IL.
[6] Ibid.

but if the intended audience is God, then aspects of theater will take a secondary role.[7] The implication here is that there is a thin line between worship and theater, and we need to be careful about violating it.

Michael J. Brown says that worship is a way of acknowledging the worthiness of God and God's vision for the world. Singing then, in the context of worship, is not just performance. Rather, it is recognizing and agreeing with God's vision for his creation. Through music and worship, we commit ourselves to participating in God's vision of what we can be in our daily walk with Him.[8]

Given the prevailing styles of music and worship, a reasonable question for us then is whether God's vision for our walk with Him varies with prevailing styles or even vice versa? Thinking in terms of social, cultural, spiritual, and relational realities, does God's vision for our "deeper life" fulfilment vary with our approach to music and worship? Shouldn't our music and worship ministry be judged by Sunday morning performance in service and how it commits Christians to be change agents in a world where most people are in need of an experience of reconciliation with Jesus?

Worship is not only what we do in congregational assembly, and differential approaches cannot substitute for hearts that are right with God. The righteousness of our hearts sanctifies whatever our approach is to music in worship.

Worship is an ongoing practice of communicating with God. It is more than articulating silently or vocally a list of requests. Worshipping God deepens our relationship with Him, and after telling Him what we desire, we ought to reflect on His concerns for us. "Real worship," says Brown, "is a dialog, a two-way conversation between God and us through proclamation, scripture reading, prayer and song."[9]

---

[7] Abington, 193.
[8] Ibid.
[9] Ibid.

Rodney A. Teal lays out for us some aspects of the experience we call worship as follows:

- Worship is a deliberate act directed to God (John 4:24).
- Worship is the grateful surrender of self (will, intellect, and emotion). God may direct us to do things that make no sense to us, but we need to be obedient by faith, recognizing that His ways and thoughts are not like our ways and thoughts (Isa 55:9).
- Worship is a response to the "God-hood" of God. Worship comprises the root "worth" (which means "value" and the suffix "ship" which means "the state of." In worship, we ascribe worth to God (Matthew 2:11).
- Worship necessarily includes sacrifice. When Abraham went to the mountain to sacrifice Isaac, he told his servants to wait while he and Isaac went to worship (Genesis 22:5). No Christian will ever be asked to lay his or her life or another person's life down in an act of sacrifice. A sacrifice is now more than a gift of convenience.[10] Actually, a sacrifice requires that one gives up something that one owns, values, and needs for one's self, but gives it anyway to another who has a greater need. In any event, we are only stewards of the things we claim to be our own. In making a biblical sacrifice we transcend giving of valuable things—we give of ourselves (Romans 12:1).

African American Music and Worship

Historically, the music and worship of African Americans are a functional outgrowth of their experiences living in a racist society. Black emigrants from Africa and the West Indies especially who are totally oblivious of what it means to live with minority status will soon discover that racism is no respecter of black national

---

[10] Ibid, 550.

or geographical origin. Such emigrants usually identify with the religious organization of their emigrant membership.

James Abington has written on hymnody in the African American church. He suggests that current musical genres grew out of folk spirituals to black meter music, to prayer and praise hymns, to improvised Euro-American hymns, hymns by African American writers, traditional and contemporary Gospel music, and to praise and worship music.[11] Thomas A Dorsey (1899–1893) is cited as the father of gospel music, in some ways similar to the gospel hymns of Sankey and Moody.

Rev. Wyatt T. Walker has described gospel music as religious folk music that identifies with the social circumstances of black Americans and an individual expression of the collective predicament in religious context.[12]

There has been criticism of gospel music holding that songwriters composed songs based upon their personal theologies and experiences rather than on a known official theology. However, in *Songs of Zion*, William B. McClain protests that the gospel song does not express the theology of the academy, university, or seminary—but rather a theology of experience, imagination, grace, and survival.[13]

In *The Spirituals and the Blues*, James Cone suggests that black music is unity music in that it unites joy and sorrow, love and hate, and hope and despair of black people, moving them in the direction of total liberation.[14] Continuing, Cone holds that black music is functional in that it is directly related to the consciousness of the black community. As well, black music is an artistic rebellion against the "humiliating deadness of Western culture, rejecting white cultural values while affirming the political otherness of black people."[15] Black music possesses a theological thrust as claimed by Dr. Cone,

---

[11] Abington, James, "Hymns in African American Churches," *Readings in African American Church Music*, vol. 2, GIA Publications Inc. 2014, Chicago, IL, 130.
[12] Ibid, 132.
[13] Ibid, 133.
[14] Ibid.
[15] Ibid.

and it presents a theological/political initiative by invoking God's Spirit to motivate toward unity and self-determination.

The main message about hymns sung in African American church worship is about lifting up the centrality of Jesus in the worship experience. Our historical and contemporary Messiah Jesus in His earth-based ministry exemplified trust and confidence, praise and adoration, and humility and obedience.

From the writings of some black authors already quoted, one can come to the conclusion that the singing of black folks at work and at worship achieves a connecting of the sacred and secular dimensions of their life experiences. It is not unlikely that both the oppressed and the oppressors are influenced by God's intervention in human affairs through folk singing and spirituals. It is believed that singing sets the human spirit free, thereby releasing the power of the Holy Spirit's presence with God's people at worship.

Preaching the Word is indispensable to black worship. It usually focuses on Jesus as a liberating power among worshippers. The slave preacher would on occasion claim that God told him that freedom was just around the corner; therefore, worshippers had to remain patient if they wanted to receive their five acres and a mule. Based upon the slave owner's monitoring of the slave preacher's leadership, it was not unusual for a slave owner to demand more praying than preaching on the possible assumption that preaching breeds factions but praying causes devotion.[16]

It should come as no surprise that African American church worship would embrace themes like tribulation, comfort, consolation, assurance, holding on, judgment, and eschatology (how the world will end).[17] Richard Wright said that black people's churches are where they dip their tired bodies in cool springs of hope, where they recover their wholeness and humanity in spite of the blows of harsh life existence.

Abingdon has been careful to supply information on the

---

[16] Ibid.
[17] Ibid, 139.

development of African American hymnals since the Second Vatican Council. "Yes Lord" (1987) was the first official hymnal of the Church of God in Christ authored by Bishop Charles H. Mason in Memphis, Tennessee. This authorship breaks with the past in the sense that in its collection of fifty songs with accompaniment, careful attention is given to the primacy of instruments in the Pentecostal tradition. It contains popular hymns, gospel hymns and songs, spirituals, and hymns from other writers, such as Andre Crouch.

"Songs of Zion" sprung from the 1973 "Consultation on the Black Church" in Atlanta and was made available to United Methodist churches. *Come Sunday: The Liturgy of Zion* was edited by William B. McClain and published in 1990 by Abingdon Press. This songbook underscores the importance of Sunday in the black community. The African American Heritage Hymnal published in 2001 was an overdue worship resource detailing the rich musical diversity of African American Protestant churches.

Total Praise: Songs and Other Worship Resources for Every Generation (2011) was copublished by GIA Publications and the Sunday School Publishing Board of the National Baptist Convention USA. Its predecessor was the *Baptist Standard Hymnal* published in 1961. This publication includes hymns of all styles, including praise and worship music from 2001–2010 by composers such as Kurt Karr, Israel, Melissa Haughton, and Kirk Franklin.

Lead Me Guide Me: An African American Catholic Hymnal (2012) comprises African American Church Music appropriate for Catholic Worship.[18] The West Angeles Church of God in Christ Mass Choir became the model for African American church praise and worship.

This sector of this chapter will now close with a hopefully appropriate quote from Abingdon's writing:

> When each member departs the sanctuary worship, he/she should have a mindset vowing to say and do

---

[18] Ibid, 141–143.

in the words of Thomas A. Dorsey. "I'm going to live the life I sing about in my song" as the African American Church continues to "Lift Every Voice and Sing" remembering and affirming that "If it had not been for the Lord on My Side, Where would I be?"

Afrocentric and Eurocentric Paradigms

Afrocentric-inspired music and worship in black worship experience have their origin in the east and west central regions of the African continent. The long history of apartheid—installed and cruelly maintained by the powerful minority Dutch Afrikaans in South Africa—was finally upended with the release of Nelson Mandela from twenty-seven years of imprisonment followed by his democratic election as the first black South African head of state in 1994. Black South Africans share full participation in Afrocentric music and worship.

Eurocentric-inspired music and worship originated in Europe and represents a belief in interpreting the world in terms of European and Anglo-American values and experiences. Classical music in the United Kingdom of Great Britain and Ireland came into existence in 1801 and inherited the European classical forms that were greatly expanded in the nineteenth century.[19]

Keith Burton, associate professor in the School of Religion at Oakwood University, recalls a passionate if not agitated spirit toward the continuing influence of Eurocentrism in some aspects of church life, mainly music and worship. His passion seemed to have come to a during the general conference in July 2015. The audience seemed to be greatly moved and inspired by classical anthems and rose to their feet at the rendering of Handel's "Hallelujah Chorus."[20] Of

---

[19] WWW.//en.wikipedia.org, "Classical Music of the United Kingdom," 1.
[20] Burton, Keith, "Ethnocentrism: Maintaining Culture at the General Conference Session" of the Pastoral Evangelism and Leadership Council, July 2015, 1.

course, rising to one's feet during this rendition has been a traditional act of courtesy in remembrance of the British queen who rose to her feet in appreciation during the rendering of Handel's signature composition. Whether by tradition or stirred emotional outpouring of appreciation, it would have made no difference to Burton. He has a case to make in regard to Eurocentric musical content being delivered in the context of an assembly that is Afrocentric in musical taste. He may have felt that this virtually imposed Eurocentric taste on the instant occasion may be suggesting that Afrocentric taste has not yet been legitimated.

A succession of songbooks from 1886 through 1985 and beyond comprises a majority of songs written in a white Anglo-Saxon European style of worship, and the only twentieth-century song in the church's hymnal was "Because He Lives" composed by the Gaithers.[21]

Burton's commentary gets even more scathing.

> Heaven is expected to adjust to the prevailing social cultural context and may be even compelled to move closer to the classical anthems of Europe, while African, Asian, Latino, and Caribbean cultures must move toward the music and worship expectations of the imperial master when told to do so.[22]

Afrocentric music and worship having been addressed in the previous section of this chapter, The Eurocentric genre now needs to be addressed perhaps more objectively.

The Eurocentric approach dates back to Germany, England, Switzerland, Scotland, and the Netherlands. They interpreted non-European histories and cultures from a European perspective, which implies the superiority of European culture, often referred to as

---

[21] Ibid, 2.
[22] Ibid, 3.

European exceptionalism. It began to thrive during early sixteenth-century development and domination of colonial empires and accelerated during the scientific revolution. The earliest and main exponent of Eurocentrism was John Calvin who held that "good teaching is an antidote to medieval superstition." He was supported by Zwingli who was ardently dismissive of singing, organs, and visual images. This mechanized European culture was contrasted with traditional hunting, farming, and herding societies with the implication of its superior standing among cultures.[23]

During the early modern period, the "European Miracle" was typified by the revival of learning (Renaissance), age of discovery, age of reason, capitalism, industrialization, and colonial empires. In the nineteenth century, Europe dominated world trade and world politics. High value was placed on learned clergy and hymnody traditions. American-based successors are Reformed American Baptists, Episcopalians, and Presbyterians. They lay substantial emphasis on being elegant, formal, and majestic, while placing high value on order, dignity, and awe.

Reaction against the sustained ascendency of Eurocentrism was not to be unexpected since many non-European cultures, nations, and societies began to envisage a revolution of rising expectations. As it has turned out, this non-European reaction was not outright rejection but rather a sort of compatible accommodation. Here are some traditions that grew out of Europe. The black clergy shirt with white tab was the garb of upper-class Englishmen during the nineteenth century. The long white robe was worn by upper-class men and deacons in ancient Rome. Black gowns were the garb of scholars in medieval Europe. Thoughtful commentary in more modern times would suggest that what was perceived as European superiority was only the provision of a model for the world at large.

In the fields of Music and Worship, there appears to be a similar type of accommodation. What was formerly the primary European

---

[23] Duck, Ruth C., *Worship [for the Whole People of God: Vital Worship for the 21st Century*, Westminster John Knox Press, Louisville, Kentucky, 2013, 49–50.

production of anthems, cantatas, oratorios, and classical concerts still enjoy contemporary presentation. Anglican writers of *High Church Hymns*, John W. Peterson and Ralph Carmichael, developed gospel music "by creating new gospel songs based on secular musical styles."[24]

The Keswick Factor (England)

From its beginning, Keswick has engaged music and worship as necessary adjuncts to the preaching and teaching of the biblical message. At the first Keswick convention in 1875, there were "services in song,"[25] conceivably inspired by Moody and Sankey campaigning with their rousing gospel singing in England. The singing of gospel hymns led by a choir became a substantial part of convention worship experience. Since then, there have been considerable changes in the form of worship as well as the choice of hymns and songs. These changes have been influenced by various changes in the church at large, especially in the Anglican/Catholic sectors of the worshipping community.

Inasmuch as the Keswick Convention is essentially British in origin, its development has been heavily impacted by Moody and Sankey and by Fanny Mae Crosby, the American author of more than eight thousand hymns. The song "Hold the Fort for I Am Coming," written by the Chicagoan Phillip Bliss, earned the plaudits of the great nineteenth-century Christian social reformer Lord Shaftsbury when he said that the singing of "Hold the Fort for I am Coming" confirmed an inestimable blessing on the British Empire."[26]

Another songwriting pair of American musicians, Hanna and Robert Pearsall Smith, introduced a songbook in 1875 declaring that the attitude of praise is always a conquering position. Since we have

---

[24] Whaley, Vernon M., *Understanding Music and Worship in the Local Church*, Evangelical Training Association, Wheaton Illinois 2002, 48–49.
[25] *Full Salvation: Keswick and Worship*, chapter 5, Excerpt from "Transforming Worship," 83.
[26] Ibid, 84.

commenced by praise, we shall end by glorious victories.[27] It should be noted that these songs and choruses of American origin received their share of criticism by critics who found them "too sentimental or lacking in dignity."[28] It is equally noteworthy that Keswick thinkers held that the prevailing type of songs and choruses were not intended for entertainment but were "to express trust in God and a more joyful experience of his goodness."[29]

The British and Keswick with their version of Fanny Crosby (Frances Ridley Havergal) authored the forever and universal contemporary "Take My Life and Let It Be" and "Who Is on the Lord's Side." She also authored "Like a River Glorious," which underscored the convention's theme of experiencing God's peace:

> Stayed upon Jehovah
> Hearts are fully blessed,
> Finding as He promised
> Glorious peace and rest.

For most insiders and observers, the capstone message of Keswick has been practical preaching of the biblical Gospel message with a view to igniting a deeper spiritual life impact. It must be noted that songs, hymns, and choruses are not employed only for the purpose of giving ancillary vocal exercise or performance display. The choice and use of hymns have been intentionally designed to corroborate preaching themes like holiness, faith, consecration, fullness of the Holy Spirit, and the Second Coming of Christ.

Historical hymns and spiritual songs have the power to teach and induce memories of mainline biblical doctrines. The spirituality of Keswick has been manifested in the hymns sung at the convention. They have the strong potential to assist transformation, resulting in a deeper level of spiritual fervor. It was believed that "experiences

---

[27] Ibid, 85.
[28] Ibid.
[29] Ibid.

of gloom and stress in Christian life would be followed eventually because of God's love, by light, calm, and joy."[30]

Another character of Keswick hymnody was a belief that salvation in Christ was not just a past event, and that it continued into present and future deliverance from the power of sin. That belief sent a clear message that spiritual transformation was linked to hymnodic themes of the 1970s. By 1981, choruses were regarded as being too repetitious and therefore lacking in biblical content. Almost simultaneously, Keswick hymns began to lift up the theme of the Holy Spirit as the agent who immersed the Christian into deeper life and deeper rest. The convention laid great emphasis on the fullness of the Spirit expressed in lines like:

> My all is on the altar
> I'm waiting for the fire;
> I'm waiting, waiting, waiting
> I'm waiting for the fire.

One contemporary evangelical hymn addresses the issue of full surrender to the Spirit as follows:

> Is your all on the altar of sacrifice laid?
> Your heart does the Spirit control?
> You can only be blessed, and have peace and sweet rest
> As you yield Him your body and soul.

In alignment with emphasis on the mission and role of the Holy Spirit was a desire to make worship more contemporary by using simple language. The American counterpart to making worship more contemporary would more likely be minimized use of traditional hymns and instruments as well as substantial use of technology to produce sounds and lighting effects supplemented by the keyboard and the Hammond B3 organ. There is no question that the latter

---

[30] Ibid, 87.

two instruments can be played delightfully, but they still lack the liturgical beauty of the well-played pipe organ.

In keeping with the desire for simplified language, one hymn that transitioned into the 1930s and encompassed nine verses of repetitive vocalization of "Power" was:

> T'is the very same power,
> T'is the very same power,
> That they had at Pentecost,
> T'is the power, the power
> T'is the power that Jesus promised should come down.[31]

As of 1881, and in process of time, sentiments began to emerge that ran counter to repetition and visual images but lifted up the need for alternative biblical content. In the midst of changes in approaches to music and worship, there seemed to be intentional "reining in" in the service of underscoring and preserving Keswick's original commitment to maintaining strong biblical, exegetical, and expository treatment of the biblical text. By the middle of the twentieth century (1950 and beyond), the convention was characterized by diversity of nationality, ethnicity, socioeconomic status, and differential spiritual experiences. Hymns were sung for as long as forty-five minutes before the start of tent meetings.

The spirituality of Keswick became mainstream evangelical, which may not have sat very well with all sectors of the diverse groups of believers. Some began to articulate greater weight to holy living than to hymn singing. Some felt that the desire for freedom of worship was creating confusion. There was fear that the convention was on its way to losing its spiritual tone. Others accused the movement of failing to sing the right kind of hymns and relaxing into sentimental and inappropriate passivity,[32] therefore lacking in

---

[31] Ibid, 91
[32] Ibid, 93.

"virile Christianity."[33] As if that was not enough, some held that the former role of women, especially hymn writers, had diminished and that female spirituality was no longer fashionable. This change in attitude precipitated revision of the current hymnal, resulting in the removal of hymns that were judged too subjective, having been laced with ecstatic content.

During the twentieth century, the evangelical wing of Keswick inspired biblical preaching as primary in worship while the Anglo Catholics espoused the Eucharist as central to worship. By 1930, Keswick was perceived as a movement that was lacking in exciting promise. However, a breakthrough came when the singing of "When I Survey the Wondrous Cross" brought back memories of prior commitment to transformation during the convention.

Then came the controversial proposal for a United Communion Service at the convention under the banner of "All One in Christ Jesus." In 1925, the Keswick Council agreed to manifest love and unity in a united service of Communion.[34] The Brethren movement, which had become a significant presence by 1930, observed weekly Communion with as many as seven hundred attendees. They looked askance at Keswick's inclusion of clergy in observing Communion. In 1934, Keswick agreed to permit the Brethren to observe Communion in a Keswick facility—but not under the auspices of the convention. Keswick remained cautious while observing the Brethren and Anglican denomination pursuing their own approaches to Communion.

The first Keswick Communion was held in 1928 when clergy and laity participated in what turned out to be a non-ritualized service of worship. By 1959, approximately five thousand people exemplified evangelical unity by observing Communion at the convention and with the use of the existing Keswick hymnal.

The Second World War interrupted Keswick's continuity, but at its resumption in 1946, a new Keswick hymnbook produced just

---

[33] Ibid.
[34] Ibid, 98.

prior to the war was used for the first time. This new hymnbook attempted to bridge the gap between the older and newer hymns. Dr. Fullerton's hymn "I Cannot Tell Why He Whom Angels Worship" earned commendation for exemplifying what it means to sing in the Spirit.

From the 1940s through the 1960s and beyond, the hymn "Full Salvation" with its message of victory over sin has been lustily sung at Keswick Conventions around the world. The South Florida Keswick—under the exuberant song leadership of Dr. David Corbin—has been singing "Full Salvation" since its inception. In 2016, there was an attempt to sing two other Keswick-originated hymns in two of four evening services of celebration. As it turned out, "Full Salvation" was preemptively sung three out of four times, which testifies to the powerful claim of "Full Salvation" on the hearts and minds of Keswick celebrants.

Although there are differences of opinion regarding the use of new paradigms, the Keswick brand of worship has remained one of Keswick's distinctive paradigm. From the 1940s through the 1960s, its form of worship has remained virtually unchanged. The organ was replaced by the piano and solo renditions in the interest of a more upbeat singing tempo. However, the organ was reintroduced to supplement the piano followed by inclusion of the violin and solo renditions. In 1960, there was a swing toward shorter choruses in preference to hymns. However, as of 1975, a choir was trained to sing the hymns while the congregation sang choruses.

Some exponents for helpful changes in contemporary worship must have questioned how long before hymns would be replaced by choruses. However, with the rapid growth of multimedia and PowerPoint packaged for worship, praise and worship has been used as a platform for contemporary worship. Hymnals have been abandoned in favor of overhead and video projectors with lyrics on a screen. Choirs have been abandoned, and bands consisting of three-to-six-member ensembles called praise teams use electronic keyboards.

The South Florida Keswick Experience

The South Florida Keswick is a diverse community of Islanders and Afro-Americans with Jamaicans in the largest numbers. It is fair to say that the South Florida Keswick Convention had its beginning in the minds and spiritual desires of persons who have been blessed through involvement with Keswick in Jamaica and other islands of the Caribbean. Chief among them is Pastor Gerry Gallimore, a " prince in the pulpit" and a preaching veteran of Keswick conventions across the English-speaking Caribbean. Under his chairmanship and with the supportive collaboration of several ecumenical pastors from Broward and Dade Counties, what started as a one Sunday night Keswick assembly has germinated and blossomed into an annual Wednesday-through-Sunday convention that has outgrown its accommodation at Metropolitan Baptist Church and obtained accommodation at the more spacious Cooper City Church of God.

Under the administration and guidance of the Keswick Council, which is comprised of incumbent and retired but serviceable pastors, South Florida Keswick has some distinctive and unique features. The Keswick Council of pastors ensures active promotion of the convention in their congregations. This collegially, spiritually, and socially bonded community of planners meets nine times each year, and friendship, love, trust, and camaraderie lift up the counsel of Jesus "that we all may be one as the Father and I are one." We expect that South Florida Keswick will continue to bring distinguished Bible teachers who have tested mastery of the expositor's craft. That approach to preaching is certain to deepen Christian living.

In Chairman Gallimore's heart is a yearning to see a full auditorium each night of the convention as well as "to see younger people 'owning' Keswick as a feature in their lives in the way many of us older ones 'owned' it in our youth."

Another exceptional feature of South Florida Keswick is its hundred-voice choir drawn from participating churches. The choir leads with choral renditions under the baton of Sister Sheila Miller, a professionally trained church musician and singer. The Keswick Council's invitation to Mrs. Miller to take charge of music for the convention was received "with great honor," considering that of all the capable choir directors in the ecumenical community, she was the chosen director. She has a record of serving thirty-five years as music director at Parkway Baptist Church. Her greatest joy has been choosing music for the choir and working with some fine musicians who are excited about serving in the Keswick ministry. She worked with these choristers in a continual music workshop that facilitated a smooth transition into the Keswick choir.

In managing choral ministry, Mrs. Miller insists on her musicians' dedication and commitment and being authentic Christians who believe in and live the message about which they sing. In choosing music, there is unavoidable reliance upon music that projects a thematic story of Christian witness and deeper spiritual living. All told, the music and worship ministry of South Florida Keswick has been riveting and exciting—whether the genre of renditions is classical (Eurocentric) or gospel music and spirituals (Afrocentric). The impact of music on South Florida Keswick has provided an inspiring dimension to our striving for deeper spiritual lifestyle.

Conclusion

It seems fair to observe that neither black theology, music nor worship (Afrocentric) nor theology of the academy, university, or seminary (Eurocentric) has genetic tracking. Either is more an issue of cultural cleavage, each manifesting its own unique beauty, dignity, and potential to ignite a genuine spirit of praise and worship. One might hold to one's preference, depending on one's differential taste.

It is a point of achieved spiritual health that Christendom in the United States is manifesting a comingling of what we might call "black Eurocentrism" and "white Afrocentrism" in that neither is frozen in its own historical rooting. Black vocal and instrumental musicians have already mastered Eurocentric skills, and white choirs have been known to virtually master black gospel music, which suggests that leaders of music and worship should be seeking to be more complementary than dominant in their approaches to pleasing the divine author of all music and worship in Keswick communities worldwide.

Let God be praised—and Keswick say, "Amen!"

Bibliography

Abingdon, James. *Readings in African American Church Music: Hymns in African American Churches.* Chicago: GIA, 2001.

Burton, Keith. *Ethnocentrism: Maintaining Culture at the General Session of the Pastoral, Evangelism, and Leadership Council.* Huntsville, 2015.

Cone, James. *The Spirituals and the Blues.* New York: Orbis Books, 1991.

Duck, Ruth C. *Worship for the Whole People of God: Vital Worship for the 21st Century.* Westminster: John Knox Press, 2013.

Jones, Mary D. *My All is on the Altar.* New York: W.C. Palmer Jr. 1869.

Mc Lain, William. *Come Sunday: The Liturgy of Zion.* Abingdon Press: 1990.

Price, Charles W., and Ian W. Randal. *Transforming Keswick.* OM Publishing: 2004.

e, Ellen G. 1Its Role, Qualities and Influence, by the 1972 Task Force on Philosophy of Music. Silver, Spring, Md 1972.

"Classical Music in the United Kingdom, early 19C." Accessed May 2017. Available from Wikipedia.org.

"Civil War Lyrics/Hold the Fort," Civil War Music. 1864. Available from www.civilwarheritagetraiks.org/civil-war-music/HoldtheFort.

"Music in the Old Testament: A Brief History of Music to David," 1958. Available from http//.summit.org. Faul, George L.

Who Is Reginald G. Smith?

Rev. Dr. Reginald G. Smith is the first son of parents who were among the first persons to be trained by American missionaries for leadership in the Church of God ministry in Jamaica.

Pastor Reggie received his education at Mico Teachers Training College in Kingston, Jamaica; Anderson University in Anderson, Indiana; New York University, Graduate School of Social Work; Union Theological Seminary in New York and Barry University, Graduate School of Philosophy and Theology in Miami.

Dr. Smith has served in senior pastoral ministry for thirty-two years: five in Harlem and twenty-seven in Florida. In 1980, he launched the Church of God of West Broward in Plantation, Florida, and led that church until he retired in 2007. His wife and partner in ministry, Carol Ann, went to her eternal reward in 2014.

Although Pastor Reggie has retired from official congregational care, he has continued to serve the ecumenical church as a preacher, seminar leader, and a resource person to churches seeking to recruit pastoral successors. He has served on the National Board of Christian Education of the Church of God, the Program Committee of the National Association of the Church of God, ministers chairman and credentials member of the Florida State Association of the Church of God, and member of the South Florida Keswick Council.

Pastor Smith has two sons, Courtney and Reginald Todd, as well as two grandchildren, Courtney Jr. and Kendall, a daughter-in-law, Andrea, and an adopted daughter, Janice. Following divine leading, he married Bernadette Bell, a happy wife and wonderful woman of God.

Chapter 7

Empowered to Forgive: Forgiving Myself
Kate Quelch

(This essay is a revised version of a sermon presented at ChristWay Baptist Church's Women's Conference in 2017 by Kate Quelch, the lone female member of the South Florida Keswick Council).

For purposes of our deliberation let us build our argument around a New Testament text, Matthew 6:14–15 (KJV):

> For if ye forgive men their trespasses, your Heavenly Father will also forgive you. But, if ye forgive not men their trespasses, neither will your Father forgive your trespasses.

Forgive, as defined by Oxford Dictionary, means to stop feeling angry or resentful toward someone for an offense, flaw, or mistake; cancel (a debt); used in polite expressions as request to excuse or regard indulgently one's foibles, ignorance, or impoliteness.

In looking at the word *offense*, synonyms such as *trespass* and *sin* immediately jump out at me for it denotes a rather serious infraction and the ultimate need for forgiveness, whereas, in comparison, the words *flaw* and *mistake* denote somewhat inherent and/or unintentional infractions.

Additionally, wherein we all can recall situations when we've had to draw upon the full meaning of the word *forgive*, I believe it is fair to say that, generally speaking, when we think about the need to forgive, the first defined point not only comes to our minds, but it rightly conjures up our feelings, that is, our need to stop feeling angry or resentful toward someone for an offense, flaw, or mistake. This point, I believe, is the crux of the matter that is, to change one's negative attitude toward the person who has wronged you.

Join me as we contemplate an even more critical component of forgiveness, an area that is often ignored but which plays an important role in the challenge of getting past the offending experience. I have chosen to focus on the matter of "forgiving myself." I chose this topic because there was a time in my life when I needed to forgive myself—or so I thought—and I suspect that there are others who, like me, have also felt this way and that there are some of us who are currently feeling this way.

What exactly do we mean when we say, "I need to forgive myself"? Do we literally mean what we say? Do we truly believe that we can actually forgive ourselves? To be honest, I believe that we do literally mean what we say, and not only that, but we actually believe what we say!

Admittedly, it didn't take me long to make this conclusion, for this premise comes as no surprise to us. Most, if not all, of us have heard it uttered before by family, friends, and colleagues. We hear it voiced on popular television shows as well as by various preachers. So often has this premise been uttered that it has become a prevalent viewpoint, and that we are considering it right now is proof enough that it is a current issue. Indeed, some of us have even moved from feeling as if we needed to forgive ourselves to literally having that little talk with ourselves wherein we convincingly say, "I forgive myself for whatever the offense might have been."

In confronting this important issue, the Lord revealed a truth to me by speaking one word into my spirit, and that word is *forgiven*. This word literally stopped me in my tracks and has channeled my thoughts into a whole new direction.

Despite the fact that we can all relate to the feeling of wanting to forgive ourselves, I respectfully submit to you that, in essence, this premise is untrue and that there is really no such thing as forgiving myself.

Now, I know that I have probably raised a few eyebrows and that some of you perhaps disagree with my statement, because I too was shocked when I received this revelation. But, upon reflection, who among us can forgive ourselves for the offenses we commit or for the offenses that have been committed against us? No one can! Neither you nor I can forgive ourselves, for the Word of God tells us in Mark 2:7 and Luke 5:21 that "no one can forgive sins, but God alone!"

The text at the beginning of this essay clearly and succinctly identifies four supreme truths:

1. We all commit trespasses.
2. We all need forgiveness.
3. If we forgive others, our heavenly Father will forgive us.
4. If we do not forgive others, our heavenly Father will not forgive us.

Although precise and powerful on its own, our text also emphasizes the context under which it falls, for it is preceded by the portion of scripture that is known as the Lord's Prayer, which we know is the manner in which Jesus taught His disciples to pray. The Lord's Prayer, among other pleas, petitions our heavenly Father to "forgive us our trespasses, as we forgive those who trespass against us." It is unambiguous and, like our text, clearly identifies not only the *need* for forgiveness but also the *criteria* for forgiveness.

The fact that Jesus reiterated the need and criteria for forgiveness in our text leads me to conclude that forgiveness is not arbitrary, but that it is a vital component of our lives. I have come to believe that it is akin to the very air we breathe for we cannot live without it! For without it, left to our own devices, we would be men and women most miserable: filthy and vile to the core and of utterly no good use to God or man. We know this to be true for the Bible tells us in Psalm 51:5, that "we were born in sin and shaped in iniquity," and in Romans 3:23, that "all have sinned, and come short of the glory of God. This fact is further born out in Romans 5:12–14, where we see that it was through Adam's disobedience to God, that sin entered into the world. Thus, Adam became a sinner, and consequently all his descendants inherited his sinful nature.

Although this reality is grim, the Bible goes on to tell us of a more excellent reality. For just as through one man did sin enter the world, so too, through the obedience of one man, that is, Jesus Christ, is the gift of righteousness made available.

For if, by the trespass of the one man, death reigned through that one man, how much more will those who receive God's abundant provision of grace and of the gift of righteousness reign in life through the one man, Jesus Christ!

Consequently, just as one trespass resulted in condemnation for all people, so also one righteous act resulted in justification and life for all people. For just as through the disobedience of the one man the many were made sinners, so also through the obedience of the one man the many will be made righteous. (Romans 5:17–19).

Righteous, as defined by Webster's Dictionary, is to be "free from guilt or sin." So then, what is this gift of righteousness? Simply stated, it is "to be right with God," deemed "free from guilt or sin." In other words: *forgiven*.

This gift of righteousness seems almost too good to be true, but it is absolutely true. But as true as it is, there is only one way for me and you to possess it, and that is for us to first believe in and accept Jesus as our Lord and Savior for it is in Him and through Him that God's gifts are commended toward us. My favorite scripture, John 3:16, perfectly bears this out:

> For God so loved the world, that he gave his only begotten Son, that whosoever believeth in him should not perish, but have everlasting life.

So now we return to the concept, *forgiven*, which is the core of this essay. Having accepted Jesus as my Lord and Savior, I boldly declare that I am forgiven. Not only can I declare it, but so can you, that is, if you have accepted Jesus as your Lord and Savior. If, on the other hand, you have not accepted Jesus as your Lord and Savior, you have the opportunity to do so today, and you too will then be able to boldly declare that you are indeed forgiven.

I must confess to you that I am deeply challenged by this very discussion because it means that I have to yield my stubborn will and confront my unwillingness to forgive myself. Oddly enough, I have always done all the right things as a Christian, which includes praying, fasting, reading my Bible. But as I sat to write this paper, I realized that there was a brick wall, that I had not totally yielded myself to the Lord. And lest you think that this is just a sidebar, it is not, for you see, I've had to come to grips with the fact that this is important and that a lesson is meant to be learned each of us.

So, what was the issue? Recognizing that God had given me what I call a hard truth to deliver, I sought to play it down. I knew for sure that He had clearly spoken to me, but I tried to soften certain aspects by using my words instead of using the exact words He had given me. After all, who am I to tell you that there is no such thing as forgiving myself and that it is a false premise, when we've heard this spoken to us many times before. So, let's not say *false*, I reasoned, let's say *untrue*. There you go! That sounds better and more palatable, I concluded! So, it is at this point that I deem the record corrected by repealing and replacing the word *untrue* with the word *false*.

The truth is that, despite my due diligence, fear and pride had crept in. Fear because of the unfamiliar premise and territory and pride, because of my reluctance to fully yield to God, which essentially was suggesting that my words were better than God's words. Wow. Talk about the need for forgiveness! Of course, I eventually repented and asked God to forgive me. How fitting that God would allow these two words to surface for both of them are antithetical to His plans and purpose for our lives, and they both have the power to hinder and destroy us. This leads me back to my brick wall, forgiveness, and the empowering truth that God has given me.

Having established that we all sin, whether knowingly or unknowingly, and that as believers, we are forgiven, what then is our obligation when we sin? Do we dismiss it, ignore it, or simply pretend as if it never happened? God forbid! We know that we're supposed to forgive others, and we know the reason why we must forgive, but what do we do about us as individuals who committed the sin? I fully appreciate what 1 John 1:9 says: "If we confess our sins, he is faithful and just to forgive us our sins, and to cleanse us from all unrighteousness." That is our individual obligation: to confess our sins to God and to receive His forgiveness, recognizing our sins are forgiven for His name's sake (1 John 2:12).

What a sense of freedom this should give us! But sadly, we don't seem to think it's sufficient. What is it that really makes us feel the need to forgive ourselves after God has forgiven us? I suggest that it is pride, that self-indulging characteristic that makes us think that it is all about me and less about God. We know that God hates pride (Proverbs 8:28) and that pride goes before destruction, and a haughty spirit before a fall (Proverbs 16:18). Yet we inadvertently behave as if God is inept or inadequate in His forgiveness, and so we need to come alongside Him and finish His work in order to make sure that it is done properly. God forbid. I am absolutely certain that this is not our intention, but it is what we imply. We allow our minds to harbor thoughts of guilt, shame, and condemnation, and in a way, failing to embrace the truth that Jesus no longer condemns us (John 3:17). What this does is it hinders us from living our best lives and becoming all that God has created us to be. But today can be the day that we put an end to this false premise by not only rejecting it, but by leaving it behind us and embracing the divine truth, that we are indeed forgiven.

That's it. We're simply forgiven, and it does not require a multitude of words or scenarios to explain it. We get trapped and hindered by our regrets, mistakes, and various issues in life, but the Lord wants us to know that as believers, whatever our offense was, is, and will be, they are all covered under the blood of Jesus, and we can lift our heads high and walk in victory, knowing that we are indeed forgiven. In fact, He wants us to focus on the positives and not the negatives, and He wants us to walk in freedom, not constantly grappling with guilt and shame.

And above all, the Lord wants us to know that he loves us so much and has forgiven us so completely that we are free to do what he created us to do, and that is to worship Him in spirit and in truth. Simply put, to worship Him with abandon.

In closing, I have found comfort in some scriptures as I come to terms with the need to embrace the forgiveness of Jesus and not feel that I need to forgive myself in order to feel forgiven.

> As far as the east is from the west, so far hath he removed our transgressions from us (Psalm 103:12).

> Blessed are those whose transgressions are forgiven, whose sins are covered. Blessed is the one whose sin the Lord will never count against them. (Romans 4:7–8)

> And be ye kind one to another, tenderhearted, forgiving one another, even as God for Christ's sake hath forgiven you. (Ephesians 4:32)

I have found that in reflecting on scriptures such as these, I am released from any sense of condemnation after I have asked for and receive God's forgiveness. I have embraced these biblical nuggets. Truly I am pleased to know that God forgives me, and I don't have to add to that by forgiving myself.

Who Is Kate Quelch?

Kate Patricia Quelch was born and raised in Grand Turk, Turks and Caicos and is a graduate of the Turks and Caicos Business College. Kate has worked in numerous administrative and managerial positions in her native country and in the United States. Kate worked as a legal administrative assistant for more than seventeen years with the law firms of Popham Haik and Carlton Fields and is currently employed as a legal administrative assistant with the prestigious law firm of Akerman LLP, the largest law firm in Florida. Kate is an active member of ChristWay Baptist Church and currently serves as a minister of the Soul Sisters Ministry, a vibrant ministry force that aims to empower single women through the Gospel and fostering spiritual and social growth through strong and dynamic activities. Kate is the sole woman on the South Florida Keswick Council where she is a voice for the youth. She is also involved in music, evangelism, and grief-support ministries in her church and wider community.

    She is the proud mother of Narada, the doting grandmother of Adaran, and the proud aunt to Chad, whom she considers a second son. Kate relishes spending time with her family.

Chapter 8

Keswick: Effectiveness and Relevance
Clyde A. Bailey

The concept of evaluation is critical in the life of any organization that seeks to continue beyond a single occurrence or appearance. To evaluate is to attempt an objective dissection of the event or operation to identify whether the objectives were achieved and to answer questions of relevance and effectiveness. In the corporate world, we see executive management retreating at various times of the year to look at profitability, productivity, performance against competition, best practices, and usefulness. That is a diagnostic exercise that provides invaluable data that helps influence decisions regarding strategy, use of resources, setting new targets or objectives, and ensuring that the organization positions itself to improve for the sake of the stakeholders, including clientele. One can only imagine how critical the exercise of evaluation is to any military unit because the nature of their operation is determined on effectiveness in carrying out its primary activities.

This discussion is an attempt to engage in an evaluation of some sort of the South Florida Keswick Convention, something that started in 2001 when some Caribbean religious luminaries who were actively involved in the Keswick movement in their home country felt a great prompting to bring this tradition of non-divisive expository Bible teaching to this part of the United States.

Keswick, which was first started in 1875 in England through

the collaborative efforts of an Anglican priest and a Quaker pastor, saw approximately four hundred persons gathering for a series of meetings under what proved to be an appropriate theme: "All One in Christ Jesus." That theme has withstood the test of time and still serves as more than a theme; it has become the nature of Keswick. People who have significant doctrinal differences can come together because they all serve Jesus regardless of their respective styles, and they can be fed from the Word of God by erudite biblical scholars who know better than to bring religious divisiveness into this ecumenical space.

For many years, South Florida Keswick has featured a hundred-voice choir drawn from participating churches. The choir has consistently provided rich choral music at each session, and many of the more seasoned Keswick followers look forward to the feast of modern gospel music presented by this well-trained choir. In addition, the organizers have managed to attract great and outstanding Bible teachers from the English-speaking Caribbean and the United States.

In 2014, Dr. Joel Edwards, international chairman of the World Evangelical Alliance and chairman of Micah Challenge International, was the main speaker for the five-day spiritual feast. Each year, the convention board takes on the challenging task of finding a speaker who, in their estimation, can feed the flock with a good, solid conventional biblical diet that leaves them asking, "Did not our hearts burn within us?" That is the given benchmark of a good convention speaker, and if the speaker is good, then the convention is good. Or is that quite true?

Let us look more closely at South Florida Keswick Convention of 2015, 2016, and 2017 and determine if this iconic Christian confab is relevant to the times in which we are living.

May 2015 was the fourteenth celebration of the South Florida Keswick Convention. The main speaker was the distinguished Bible scholar, Rev. Dr. Edward Lewis Fogg, retired general secretary/chief executive officer of the leadership council of the Church of God in Indiana. Dr. Foggs was accompanied by his wife of sixty

For Such a Time as This

years, Joyce, and he spoke at the five nightly sessions, the Saturday morning leaders' breakfast, and at one of the participating churches on Sunday morning.

The convention, which ran from May 13 through to May 17, saw an average attendance of eight hundred each night with closer to a thousand in attendance on the last night. Each night, there was a rich presentation of choral music, vibrant praise and worship, and a simple yet profound presentation of the Word of God. In addition, a book table provided reasonably priced literature and an active media sales booth where people were able to purchase audio and video recordings of each night's services and the Saturday morning breakfast for leaders.

The Keswick Convention is organized by a team of pastors. The former president of Youth for Christ International, Dr. Gerry Gallimore, added two lunch-hour sessions in different locations across South Florida that year. Friday night took on a more youthful tone as young people from the various churches presented a full program of song, dance, and vibrant praise as part of an exciting service.

Keswick 2016 had as its featured speaker the English-born broadcaster and Bible scholar, Stuart Briscoe, and his wife, Jill Briscoe. Stuart, who has authored more than fifty books, pastored the Elmwood Church in Wisconsin for nearly thirty years and is currently heard on a daily syndicated radio show, "Telling the Truth." He and his wife—also a prolific writer—are regular conference speakers all over the globe. Stuart was the main speaker at each of the night meetings, and for the first time, South Florida Keswick hosted a women's meeting. Jill Briscoe addressed a group of approximately two hundred people on Thursday morning. Once again, the Friday night service was a mixture of youth and experience as several young people participated in the service, which had an experienced eighty-four-year-old speaker addressing the nearly nine hundred-member congregation. The final night of the crusade recorded nearly a thousand attendees.

In 2017, it was different. The speaker was local, young, and black.

Rev. Dr. Marcus Davidson, a native of Alabama, is the senior pastor of the New Mount Olive Baptist Church in Fort Lauderdale. Dr. Davidson came to Keswick with an impressive academic background capped with a doctor of ministry degree in black church leadership from the Southern Baptist Theological Seminary in Kentucky. Dr. Davidson was not a member of the Keswick cadre of renowned speakers, so his coming to South Florida Keswick Convention created some curious anticipation.

Dr. Davidson brought his own style to the pulpit. He spoke for three nights on the subject of holiness as discussed in the first chapter of Peter's first letter. The one night that he was absent, this writer filled the pulpit. It was not accidental that it was another local speaker who was called on to feed the hungry Keswick soul.

On the first night, Dr. Davidson led the congregation into a fresh understanding of how holiness ought to be expanded to cover all areas of one's life as we represent Jesus in a challenging environment. By the time we got to the final night, he had developed a reputation of being a short but succinct preacher. The Bible scholar demonstrated skills in exegesis and had the congregation asking for more. On the final night, he unveiled his skills as a powerful, erudite, Spirit-led, and charismatic preacher. The overflowing congregation was captivated by his handling of scriptures and his commitment to keeping it real.

The women's service was moved to Saturday morning, which proved to be a wise decision. That service featured a segment called "Girl Talk" with a three-member panel of women sharing the huge challenges they have faced and how their faith-based relationship with God took them over the mountains. The ladies brought a special kind of worship that morning, and the music of the event was rich and spirit-filled, which must have been a new trend. The speaker, Pat Bailey, was from the host church and unveiled a solid review of Psalm 1, focusing on the tree planted by the rivers of water. This captivating treatment of the Word was fresh and dynamic as was indicated by the tremendous response to an altar call. Keswick women cemented their claim as a serious feature of the annual convention.

At the end, the organizers gathered to assess the event, count the finances, and determine whether the convention was successful. The last clause informs our deliberation.

There are two simple questions that need to be considered as one seeks to determine the relevance of Keswick Convention. What is the goal of the convention? What is the target audience? The fact that this imported Christian festival has survived in metropolitan South Florida since 2002 suggests that there is a place for this event among Christians in that part of the United States. Each year, the organizers are challenged to find a good speaker who is proficient in expository Bible teaching and a man of good repute. They have sought to introduce to the faithful followers men of different races, ages, and denominational backgrounds. The local and international speakers are known and respected enough to be entertained in the hollowed pulpit of South Florida Keswick. For the past two years, the lineup of speakers have included women as the South Florida Keswick board introduced the women's meeting.

The first question brings us to a place of purpose: what is the goal of the convention? Historically, Keswick has always been a forum not for churches but for believers to learn biblical truths that will lead to spiritual growth. South Florida Keswick has sought to maintain that pure principle, and it would be fair to say that, since its inaugural convention in 2002, South Florida Keswick planners have tried to achieve that goal. The notion of spiritual growth is not to disregard the effect and role of the local churches; the convention is supposed to complement and supplement the efforts of the local church in bringing members to continuous and authentic growth in Christ. This is what informs the convention committee when selecting speakers because they are less concerned about popularity and notoriety than finding a speaker who is theologically sound and evangelical in orientation and who will rely solely on scriptures to craft his sermons to effectively lead to exponential growth.

How does one measure that goal? What mechanisms have the organizers employed to be able to say that the goal is achieved? Growth occurred. The 2002 convention was a one-night event, and seventeen years later, it is a four-night event. Growth occurred. Over the years, the venue has changed four times, each time reaching for a larger auditorium because of the growing number of persons attending the nightly meetings. Growth occurred. Over the past three years, the main convention sessions were streamed live, reaching a wider audience. Growth occurred. Tangible growth has occurred. However, there doesn't seem to be an objective way of determining whether spiritual growth has occurred, which is the main purpose for staging this costly spiritual event.

Pastors of participating churches are not required to report back to the committee whether they identified members of their churches who have grown spiritually because of their experiences at Keswick. The assumption is that if we stage the convention, people will come, and the fact that people attend is an acceptable yardstick to measure growth.

One could argue that, despite the fact that they have changed venues four times, more people should be attending the meetings—and more churches should be rushing to become a part of this seemingly great movement. Could it be that Keswick is more of a fixture on the church calendar, people attend because of tradition, it is a reliable forum of sound Bible teaching, and people go to the meetings based on tradition or for entertainment? The choir is good, the speaker is good, the service is good, and people leave after declaring that it was a good night. That is hardly the most effective way to determine relevance.

Purpose is something that has to be considered since the past two years included a women's service. The tradition of Keswick does not provide it, but in South Florida, the organizers thought it practical to facilitate a special session for women and served by women. It is commendable that a women's service has been added because it affords women an opportunity to hear the Word of God masterfully taught by a woman. This can be encouraging and spiritually uplifting for the women who are the backbone of the rank and file of those who support Keswick. There are more women than men in the regular convention sessions, so a women's service makes sense. The women of South Florida have had an imported speaker one year and a local speaker in the second year, each having brought strong biblical teaching to the service and proved to the organizers that such a service ought to become a part of the week's events.

This brings us to the second question: what is the target audience for South Florida Keswick? Generally speaking, the majority of people who attend the South Florida Keswick are people who used to attend a Keswick convention in the English-speaking Caribbean. The majority of those who attend are people who attend local churches that are predominantly Caribbean, led by Caribbean pastors. It is highly unusual to find a significant number of Americans in the services, and the event certainly doesn't attract other nationalities residing in South Florida.

There is also the age factor. The majority are middle-aged and older people who are familiar with the great Keswick conventions "back home," and the format has to closely resemble what they were used to in the Caribbean. Caribbean Christians are not prejudiced toward the ethnicity or race of the speaker. The main thing they insist on is that he must be skilled in breaking the Word to elicit strong "amens" throughout the sermon presentation.

Qualitatively, the speakers are outstanding. The past three years were challenging as far as speakers were concerned because the planners brought in elderly Bible scholars for two successive years. These men of great renown were way past their prime years of preaching. In 2017, they found a local young preacher who stood tall on this established platform and earned the respect of the planners and attendees. In 2015 and 2016, one sensed that the congregation was apprehensive as to whether these strong biblical teachers could hold the attention of the congregation. On each occasion, the elder statesmen proved their mettle. Foggs and Briscoe won the hearts of the seasoned Christians with their intellect and patient treatment of scriptures. Their experience served well in making them effective in communicating the message to a critical audience. Davidson was not intimidated by the Keswick culture and allowed the Holy Spirit to guide him in ministering to the seasoned Keswick audience.

Audio and video recordings of the Keswick services were in

great demand. People expressed appreciation for the way each of the men handled the Word of God. It is fair to conclude that the target audience might not have been deliberately selected, but those of Caribbean ancestry who attended the convention said they were blessed.

Is Keswick still relevant and effective? Is this annual event effective in driving people to a deeper walk with God and to display greater indications of spiritual growth? There are some issues that should be considered.

Firstly, the number of night sessions is enough to keep the Christian attendees returning, but maybe we can revisit the question of whether it is achieving its goal. If the goal is to motivate the local Christian community to more pronounced spiritual growth, then the organizers are expressing a confidence in the product—South Florida Keswick. However, the organizers could encourage the leaders of local participating churches to vigorously promote the event and get more of their members to attend.

Immediately after the convention, local church leaders could conduct evaluation sessions in their churches involving those who attended the convention. It would be encouraging to hear pastors reporting that a group of Christians started a small group Bible study to build on the spiritual effect of the convention. It would be even powerful to hear from pastors about members of their congregations who have rededicated their lives to the Lord and have become involved (or more involved) in Christian service. The board would be delighted to hear strong reports from local pastors.

In continuing the evaluation process, the organizers need to be clear about what audience they are going after. We live in a multinational and multigenerational community. South Florida is a melting pot of cultures, races, ethnicities, and denominations, and it is not wise to cater only to one group of immigrants. Strategic and modern marketing strategies need to be employed so that a wider cross-section of the Christian community can be reached with a compelling invitation. It might necessitate hiring a professional marketing group to take on the business of promoting the event.

Keswick has survived more than 130 years since its humble beginnings in the United Kingdom, and it is still drawing crowds. However, more people can be reached. South Florida has a large Hispanic community that the Keswick board has not yet tapped into. Our efforts can be extended to reach white America, migrant communities, Pentecostals, Catholics, and others. This would necessitate a large budget and launching the marketing blitz at least three months before the actual event. The marketing plan should have a built-in facility to reach across the aisle to other churches and denominations that have not previously attended the convention.

A critical plank of the marketing of the annual Bible fair, is to find a way to reach the younger generation: millennials. This demographic segment seems to be the target of most marketing efforts, so churches, manufacturers, and service providers are intentionally reaching out to this populous group. Millennials are willing to attend and participate in spiritual events, but such events have to be made attractive to them.

Dinosaur-type events such as Keswick have to be on the cutting edge of presentations because millennials want to be convinced and impressed to warrant them returning for a second service. Millennials challenge the status quo of conservative religious culture via their propensity to dress casually. They generally consider body piercing and body painting acceptable. Their music has jumped from Reformation and nineteenth-century hymns and songs to the Hillsong genre of music where the lyrics are vibrant and energetic. Millennials believe their contemporary taste in every sphere of life is the most practical way. To ignore the voice and demands of this segment of the local population is to take a huge risk because they are powerful—and they are here to stay.

In closing this chapter, the message of Keswick is the church needs a deliberate and powerful thrust aimed to foster spiritual growth. Spiritual growth will motivate Christians to be more engaged in ministry, especially to win the lost for Christ.

Keswick has to change its packaging and methodology and retain its message. Keswick must be willing to reach beyond the familiar and venture into the other sections of the community, Judea, Samaria and the uttermost parts of the world, a world that is coming to us in droves each day from all over the world. It is not unthinkable for Keswick to consider moving to much larger accommodation because great numbers will be flocking to the services. I dare to prophesy that the South Florida Keswick movement has the capacity to change. It simply needs to find the will to effect the change, knowing full well that it was raised up by God in this community for such a time as this.

Who Is Clyde A. Bailey?

Clyde A. Bailey is executive pastor at Cooper City Church of God and Director of Cooper City Family Center. He previously taught at the University of the West Indies (UWI, Mona) and Nova Southeastern University. Clyde has worked extensively in the corporate world and in the education industry in three countries. His first major publication is *Brothers (You Can) Get It Right*, and he coauthored *Lifting Our Literary Voices: An Anthology of Poetry, Short Stories, and Essays* with Ralph Hogges, Marva Hare Morris, and Indiana Robinson. In addition, he speaks at conferences and seminars and in numerous churches. He's a graduate of UWI, Mona with a bachelor's degree in sociology and master's degree in social psychology. Clyde graduated from Nova Southeastern University with a doctoral degree in family therapy. Clyde is an ordained bishop in the Church of God in Cleveland, Tennessee. He and his wife, Patricia, have one son, John-Patrick.

Epilogue

South Florida Keswick Convention
Statement of Faith

1. We believe the Bible to be the inspired, the only infallible, authoritative Word of God.
2. We believe that there is one God, eternally existent in three persons: Father, Son, and Holy Spirit.
3. We believe in the deity of our Lord Jesus Christ, in His virgin birth, in His sinless life, in His miracles, in His vicarious and atoning death through His shed blood, in His bodily resurrection, in His ascension to the right hand of the Father, and in His personal return in power and glory.
4. We believe that for the salvation of lost and sinful people, regeneration by the Holy Spirit is absolutely essential.
5. We believe in the present ministry of the Holy Spirit by whose indwelling the Christian is enabled to live a godly life.
6. We believe in the resurrection of both the saved and the lost: those who are saved unto the resurrection of life and those who are lost unto the resurrection of damnation.
7. We believe in the spiritual unity of believers in our Lord Jesus Christ.

Current Board Members

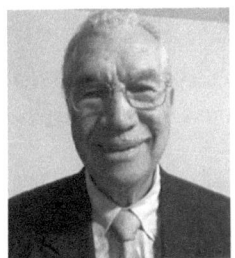

Rev. Dr. Gerry Gallimore,
Chairman and Retired Pastor, Metropolitan Baptist Church

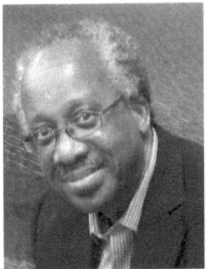

Rev. Dr. Raymond Anglin, Vice Chairman
Retired Pastor, Ascension Peace Presbyterian Church

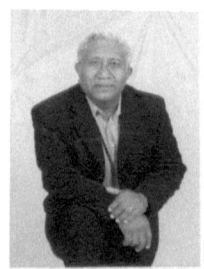

Dr. Aubrey Fredericks
Secretary, Fountainside Christian Fellowship

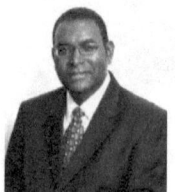

Rev. Karl Francis, Treasurer
Lead Pastor, Living Word Open Bible Church

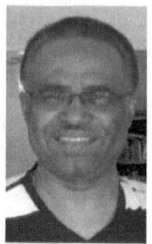

Rev. Ansel Aiken
Lead Pastor, South Florida Gospel Church

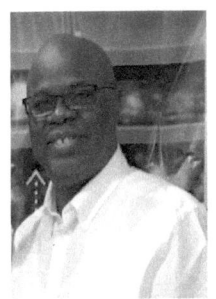

Rev. Dr. Clyde A. Bailey
Executive Pastor, Cooper City Church of God

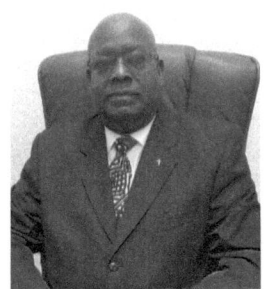

Rev. Dr. Lincoln Bowen
Lead Pastor, Lauderhill Baptist Church

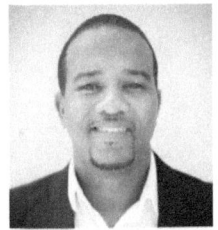

Rev. Arthur Conner Jr.
Lead Pastor, Metropolitan Baptist Church

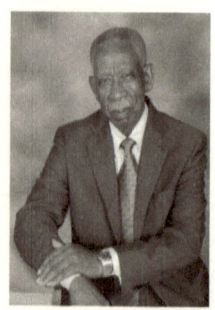

Rev. Dr. Amos Farquharson
Lead Pastor, First Baptist Church of Sunrise

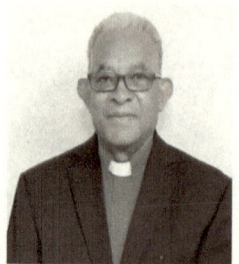

Rev. Dr. Joseph Prendergast
Lead Pastor, Evangelistic Temple

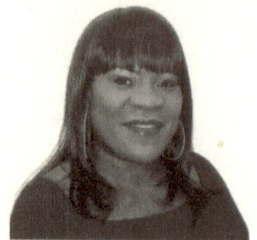

Ms. Kate Quelch
Youth Affairs, ChristWay Baptist Church

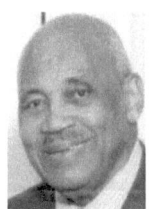

Rev. Dr. Reggie Smith
Retired Pastor

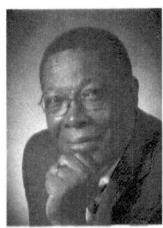

Rev. Dr. Wesley Green
Lead Pastor, ChristWay Baptist Church

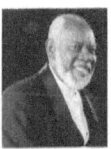

Rev. Dr. Richard Heron
Retired Pastor, MGC Worship Center

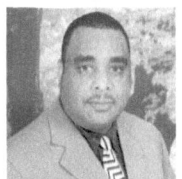

Rev. Donald Lawrence
Lead Pastor, Parkway Baptist Church

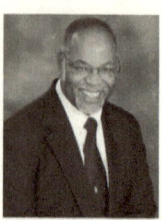

Rev. Dr. Richard Ledgister
Retired Pastor, Sierra-Norwood Baptist Church

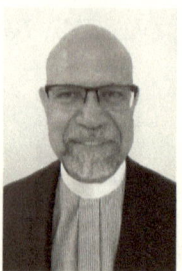

Father Horace Ward
Rector, Holy Family Episcopal Church

www.ingramcontent.com/pod-product-compliance
Lightning Source LLC
Chambersburg PA
CBHW020446220526
45464CB00002B/887